TEACHER'S PET PUBLICATIONS

PUZZLE PACK
for
Bud, Not Buddy
based on the book by
Christopher Paul Curtis

Written by
Mary B. Collins

© 2005 Teacher's Pet Publications
All Rights Reserved

The materials in this packet are copyrighted
by Teacher's Pet Publications, Inc.

These pages may be duplicated by the purchaser
for use in the purchaser's own classroom.

Copying any of these materials and distributing them
for any other purpose is a violation of the copyright laws.

© 2005 Teacher's Pet Publications, Inc.
www.tpet.com

INTRODUCTION
If you already own the LitPlan for this title, this Puzzle Pack will refresh your Unit Resource Materials and Vocabulary Resource Materials sections plus give you additional materials you can substitute into the tests. If you do not already have a complete LitPlan, these pages will give you some supplemental materials to use with your own plan. There are two main groups of materials: one set for unit words (such as characters' names, symbols, places, etc.) and one set for vocabulary words associated with the book.

WORD LIST
There is a word list for both the unit words and the vocabulary words. These lists show you which words are being used in the materials and the clues or definitions being used for those words. You may want to give students a word list with clues/definitions to help them, or you may want students to only have a word list (without clues/definitions) if you want them to work a little harder. Both are available for duplication. The word lists can also be your "calling key" for the bingo games.

FILL IN THE BLANK AND MATCHING
There are 4 each of the fill in the blank and matching worksheets for both the unit and vocabulary words. These pages can be used either as extra worksheets for students or as objective parts of a unit test. They can be done individually if students need extra help or as a whole class activity to review the material covered.

MAGIC SQUARES
The magic squares not only reinforce the material covered but also work on reasoning and math skills. Many teachers have told us that their students really enjoy doing these!

WORD SEARCH PUZZLES
The word search words go in all directions, as indicated on your answer keys. Two of the word search puzzles have the clues listed rather than the words. This makes the puzzle a little more difficult, but it reinforces the material better. Two word search puzzles have words only for students who find the clue puzzles too difficult.

CROSSWORD PUZZLES
Both unit and vocabulary word sections have 4 crossword puzzles.

BINGO CARDS
There are 32 individual bingo cards for the unit words and 32 individual bingo cards for the vocabulary words. You can use your word list as a "call list," calling the words at random and marking them off of your list as you go, or you could use the flash cards by cutting them apart and drawing the words at random from a hat (or box or whatever). To make a better review, you might ask for the definition and spelling of each word as you call it out–or you could call out the definitions and have students tell you the words they need to look for on the puzzle.

JUGGLE LETTERS
The vocabulary juggle letter game is intended to help students learn the spellings of the words. One sheet has the definitions listed on it as an extra help for students who need it or to reinforce the definitions if you choose to do so.

FLASH CARDS
We've included a set of vocabulary flash cards you can duplicate, cut, and fold for your students. Some teachers make a few sets for general use by the class; others make a set for each student. Some teachers duplicate them for each student and have the students cut & fold their own. You can cut out just the words and put them in a hat, have each student pick out one word and write the definition and a sentence for that word. Students then swap words and papers, with the next student adding a sentence of his own under the last one. You can have students swap as many times as you like. Each time the student will read the sentences written prior to his own and then add a sentence. You can cut out the words and definitions separately and play "I Have; Who Has?" Each student in the room draws a word and definition. The first student says, "I have (the name of the word). Who has the definition?" The student with the definition reads it then says, "I have (the name of the vocabulary word she has). Who has the definition?" The round continues until all words and definitions have been given.

Bud, Not Buddy Unit Word List

No.	Word	Clue/Definition
1.	AMOS	Mr. ___ locked Bud in the shed
2.	ANGELA	___ Janet; Momma
3.	BLANKET	When wrapped in it, Bud felt close to Momma
4.	BLOOD	Lefty was transporting this, so Bud thought he was a vampire
5.	BROWN	John ___; abolitionist
6.	BUD	___, Not Buddy
7.	BUGS	A cockroach crawled in his ear
8.	CALDWELL	Bud's last name
9.	CALLOWAY	Herman E. ___
10.	CAPONE	Al ___; leader of Chicago underworld
11.	CAR	Bud tried to drive Lefty's away
12.	CLARENCE	Bud's pretend name at the mission
13.	COPS	They tried to keep the men off of the train
14.	DEAD	Gone = ___ (Rule 28)
15.	DEPRESSION	HEC & The Dusky Devastators of the ___
16.	DEZA	Miss Malone
17.	DOOR	When one closes, another one opens
18.	EDDIE	Steady ___
19.	FBI	Federal Bureau of Investigation
20.	FIDDLE	HEC's instrument; a giant ___
21.	FISH	Guards at the shed door
22.	FLINT	City where Bud & Momma lived
23.	FLYERS	They had printed information about HEC and the band
24.	GRACE	Miss Thomas's first name
25.	GRANDFATHER	HEC to Bud
26.	GUN	1st part of the revenge plan was to get rid of this
27.	HERBERT	___ Hoover; President of United States
28.	HERMAN	Mr. Calloway's first name
29.	HOME	Bud's word for the orphanage
30.	HOOVER	J. Edgar ___; head of FBI for 48 years
31.	HOOVERVILLE	Cardboard town for the homeless
32.	HORNETS	The vampire bat was actually this kind of a nest
33.	JERRY	He got a foster home with girls
34.	JIMMY	Horn player who helped Bud
35.	KELLY	Machine Gun ___; gangster
36.	KLAN	Ku Klux ___; organization against equal rights; members anonymous
37.	LABOR	Police stopped Lefty looking for ___ organizers
38.	LAM	On the ___; running away
39.	LEFTY	Mr. Lewis
40.	LIBRARY	Bud looked for Miss Hill there
41.	MICHIGAN	State where Bud lived
42.	MISSION	Place where Bud got food
43.	MOMMA	She was unhappy at the Miss B. Gotten Moon Park
44.	MOON	Miss B. Gotten ___ Park
45.	PEA	Sweet ___; restaurant
46.	RAPIDS	Grand ___; where HEC lived
47.	READ	Momma ___ to Bud until he fell asleep
48.	RED	___ caps; men who handled baggage at the train
49.	RULES	___ & Things Number 328
50.	SAXOPHONE	Instrument band gave to Bud

Bud, Not Buddy Unit Word List Continued

No.	Word	Clue/Definition
51.	SEEDS	Ideas are a lot like these
52.	SHED	Where Amoses locked Bud
53.	SLEEPY	___ LaBone; Bud
54.	SLEET	Mrs. ___ was Lefty's daughter
55.	STATION	Grand Calloway ___
56.	STONES	Had numbers & letters written on them
57.	SUITCASE	It held Bud's blanket, flyer & things
58.	TEARS	Bud's had all dried up; he didn't cry often
59.	TELEGRAM	Lefty sent one to HEC, advising him of Bud's whereabouts
60.	THOMAS	Miss ___; vocal stylist who took care of Bud
61.	TRAIN	The boys wanted to hop on one going west
62.	ZOOP	Whoop, ___, Sloop!

Bud, Not Buddy Fill In The Blanks 1

_____ 1. Bud's word for the orphanage

_____ 2. They had printed information about HEC and the band

_____ 3. Bud's had all dried up; he didn't cry often

_____ 4. Sweet ___; restaurant

_____ 5. Bud's last name

_____ 6. Mr. Calloway's first name

_____ 7. When one closes, another one opens

_____ 8. Grand Calloway _____

_____ 9. ____ Hoover; President of United States

_____ 10. Horn player who helped Bud

_____ 11. Grand ____; where HEC lived

_____ 12. Bud's pretend name at the mission

_____ 13. Federal Bureau of Investigation

_____ 14. _____ & Things Number 328

_____ 15. HEC to Bud

_____ 16. Miss Thomas's first name

_____ 17. It held Bud's blanket, flyer & things

_____ 18. ____ Janet; Momma

_____ 19. Al ____; leader of Chicago underworld

_____ 20. Ku Klux ____; organization against equal rights; members anonymous

Bud, Not Buddy Fill In The Blanks 1 Answer Key

HOME	1. Bud's word for the orphanage
FLYERS	2. They had printed information about HEC and the band
TEARS	3. Bud's had all dried up; he didn't cry often
PEA	4. Sweet ___; restaurant
CALDWELL	5. Bud's last name
HERMAN	6. Mr. Calloway's first name
DOOR	7. When one closes, another one opens
STATION	8. Grand Calloway _____
HERBERT	9. _____ Hoover; President of United States
JIMMY	10. Horn player who helped Bud
RAPIDS	11. Grand _____; where HEC lived
CLARENCE	12. Bud's pretend name at the mission
FBI	13. Federal Bureau of Investigation
RULES	14. _____ & Things Number 328
GRANDFATHER	15. HEC to Bud
GRACE	16. Miss Thomas's first name
SUITCASE	17. It held Bud's blanket, flyer & things
ANGELA	18. _____ Janet; Momma
CAPONE	19. Al _____; leader of Chicago underworld
KLAN	20. Ku Klux _____; organization against equal rights; members anonymous

Bud, Not Buddy Fill In The Blanks 2

_____
_____
_____
_____
_____
_____
_____
_____
_____
_____
_____
_____
_____
_____
_____
_____
_____
_____
_____
_____

1. On the ___; running away
2. Al ____; leader of Chicago underworld
3. Bud's word for the orphanage
4. They had printed information about HEC and the band
5. Federal Bureau of Investigation
6. _____ & Things Number 328
7. Miss Malone
8. 1st part of the revenge plan was to get rid of this
9. Machine Gun ____; gangster
10. She was unhappy at the Miss B. Gotten Moon Park
11. Mr. Lewis
12. HEC & The Dusky Devastators of the _____
13. Mr. ___ locked Bud in the shed
14. Gone = ____ (Rule 28)
15. J. Edgar ____; head of FBI for 48 years
16. Cardboard town for the homeless
17. Mrs. ___ was Lefty's daughter
18. When wrapped in it, Bud felt close to Momma
19. Sweet ___; restaurant
20. Grand ____; where HEC lived

Bud, Not Buddy Fill In The Blanks 2 Answer Key

LAM	1. On the ___; running away
CAPONE	2. Al ___; leader of Chicago underworld
HOME	3. Bud's word for the orphanage
FLYERS	4. They had printed information about HEC and the band
FBI	5. Federal Bureau of Investigation
RULES	6. ___ & Things Number 328
DEZA	7. Miss Malone
GUN	8. 1st part of the revenge plan was to get rid of this
KELLY	9. Machine Gun ___; gangster
MOMMA	10. She was unhappy at the Miss B. Gotten Moon Park
LEFTY	11. Mr. Lewis
DEPRESSION	12. HEC & The Dusky Devastators of the ___
AMOS	13. Mr. ___ locked Bud in the shed
DEAD	14. Gone = ___ (Rule 28)
HOOVER	15. J. Edgar ___; head of FBI for 48 years
HOOVERVILLE	16. Cardboard town for the homeless
SLEET	17. Mrs. ___ was Lefty's daughter
BLANKET	18. When wrapped in it, Bud felt close to Momma
PEA	19. Sweet ___; restaurant
RAPIDS	20. Grand ___; where HEC lived

Bud, Not Buddy Fill In The Blanks 3

_____ 1. HEC's instrument; a giant ____

_____ 2. Miss Thomas's first name

_____ 3. A cockroach crawled in his ear

_____ 4. Miss B. Gotten ____ Park

_____ 5. ___ caps; men who handled baggage at the train

_____ 6. Machine Gun ____; gangster

_____ 7. Sweet ___; restaurant

_____ 8. Place where Bud got food

_____ 9. City where Bud & Momma lived

_____ 10. Bud's pretend name at the mission

_____ 11. 1st part of the revenge plan was to get rid of this

_____ 12. ____, Not Buddy

_____ 13. Bud looked for Miss Hill there

_____ 14. Mrs. ___ was Lefty's daughter

_____ 15. J. Edgar ____; head of FBI for 48 years

_____ 16. Ideas are a lot like these

_____ 17. Bud tried to drive Lefty's away

_____ 18. Had numbers & letters written on them

_____ 19. Federal Bureau of Investigation

_____ 20. Guards at the shed door

Bud, Not Buddy Fill In The Blanks 3 Answer Key

FIDDLE	1. HEC's instrument; a giant ____
GRACE	2. Miss Thomas's first name
BUGS	3. A cockroach crawled in his ear
MOON	4. Miss B. Gotten ____ Park
RED	5. ___ caps; men who handled baggage at the train
KELLY	6. Machine Gun ____; gangster
PEA	7. Sweet ___; restaurant
MISSION	8. Place where Bud got food
FLINT	9. City where Bud & Momma lived
CLARENCE	10. Bud's pretend name at the mission
GUN	11. 1st part of the revenge plan was to get rid of this
BUD	12. ____, Not Buddy
LIBRARY	13. Bud looked for Miss Hill there
SLEET	14. Mrs. ___ was Lefty's daughter
HOOVER	15. J. Edgar ____; head of FBI for 48 years
SEEDS	16. Ideas are a lot like these
CAR	17. Bud tried to drive Lefty's away
STONES	18. Had numbers & letters written on them
FBI	19. Federal Bureau of Investigation
FISH	20. Guards at the shed door

Bud, Not Buddy Fill In The Blanks 4

_____

_____

_____

_____

_____

_____

_____

_____

_____

_____

_____

_____

_____

_____

_____

_____

_____

_____

_____

_____

1. Guards at the shed door
2. She was unhappy at the Miss B. Gotten Moon Park
3. _____ & Things Number 328
4. Bud tried to drive Lefty's away
5. ____ Hoover; President of United States
6. Miss ___; vocal stylist who took care of Bud
7. Whoop, _____, Sloop!
8. Lefty was transporting this, so Bud thought he was a vampire
9. Bud's had all dried up; he didn't cry often
10. Mr. Lewis
11. Miss B. Gotten ____ Park
12. HEC & The Dusky Devastators of the _____
13. Had numbers & letters written on them
14. Miss Malone
15. Instrument band gave to Bud
16. It held Bud's blanket, flyer & things
17. Grand ____; where HEC lived
18. 1st part of the revenge plan was to get rid of this
19. ___ LaBone; Bud
20. Mrs. ___ was Lefty's daughter

Bud, Not Buddy Fill In The Blanks 4 Answer Key

FISH	1. Guards at the shed door
MOMMA	2. She was unhappy at the Miss B. Gotten Moon Park
RULES	3. _____ & Things Number 328
CAR	4. Bud tried to drive Lefty's away
HERBERT	5. ____ Hoover; President of United States
THOMAS	6. Miss ___; vocal stylist who took care of Bud
ZOOP	7. Whoop, _____, Sloop!
BLOOD	8. Lefty was transporting this, so Bud thought he was a vampire
TEARS	9. Bud's had all dried up; he didn't cry often
LEFTY	10. Mr. Lewis
MOON	11. Miss B. Gotten ____ Park
DEPRESSION	12. HEC & The Dusky Devastators of the _____
STONES	13. Had numbers & letters written on them
DEZA	14. Miss Malone
SAXOPHONE	15. Instrument band gave to Bud
SUITCASE	16. It held Bud's blanket, flyer & things
RAPIDS	17. Grand ____; where HEC lived
GUN	18. 1st part of the revenge plan was to get rid of this
SLEEPY	19. ___ LaBone; Bud
SLEET	20. Mrs. ___ was Lefty's daughter

Bud, Not Buddy Matching 1

___ 1. DOOR   A. Miss Malone
___ 2. LIBRARY   B. When one closes, another one opens
___ 3. LEFTY   C. J. Edgar ____; head of FBI for 48 years
___ 4. MISSION   D. Mr. Calloway's first name
___ 5. HOOVER   E. Guards at the shed door
___ 6. RULES   F. HEC & The Dusky Devastators of the _____
___ 7. HERBERT   G. Bud's last name
___ 8. COPS   H. She was unhappy at the Miss B. Gotten Moon Park
___ 9. FISH   I. Grand Calloway _____
___10. ZOOP   J. Bud tried to drive Lefty's away
___11. MOMMA   K. Miss Thomas's first name
___12. DEPRESSION   L. Bud looked for Miss Hill there
___13. CAR   M. Place where Bud got food
___14. GRACE   N. ____ Hoover; President of United States
___15. CALDWELL   O. ___ LaBone; Bud
___16. SLEEPY   P. Mrs. ___ was Lefty's daughter
___17. STATION   Q. When wrapped in it, Bud felt close to Momma
___18. DEZA   R. Mr. Lewis
___19. BLANKET   S. _____ & Things Number 328
___20. EDDIE   T. Steady ____
___21. SLEET   U. Gone = ____ (Rule 28)
___22. SUITCASE   V. Whoop, _____, Sloop!
___23. HERMAN   W. They tried to keep the men off of the train
___24. DEAD   X. It held Bud's blanket, flyer & things
___25. SAXOPHONE   Y. Instrument band gave to Bud

Bud, Not Buddy Matching 1 Answer Key

B - 1. DOOR
L - 2. LIBRARY
R - 3. LEFTY
M - 4. MISSION
C - 5. HOOVER
S - 6. RULES
N - 7. HERBERT
W - 8. COPS
E - 9. FISH
V - 10. ZOOP
H - 11. MOMMA
F - 12. DEPRESSION
J - 13. CAR
K - 14. GRACE
G - 15. CALDWELL
O - 16. SLEEPY
I - 17. STATION
A - 18. DEZA
Q - 19. BLANKET
T - 20. EDDIE
P - 21. SLEET
X - 22. SUITCASE
D - 23. HERMAN
U - 24. DEAD
Y - 25. SAXOPHONE

A. Miss Malone
B. When one closes, another one opens
C. J. Edgar ____; head of FBI for 48 years
D. Mr. Calloway's first name
E. Guards at the shed door
F. HEC & The Dusky Devastators of the _____
G. Bud's last name
H. She was unhappy at the Miss B. Gotten Moon Park
I. Grand Calloway _____
J. Bud tried to drive Lefty's away
K. Miss Thomas's first name
L. Bud looked for Miss Hill there
M. Place where Bud got food
N. ____ Hoover; President of United States
O. ___ LaBone; Bud
P. Mrs. ___ was Lefty's daughter
Q. When wrapped in it, Bud felt close to Momma
R. Mr. Lewis
S. _____ & Things Number 328
T. Steady ____
U. Gone = ____ (Rule 28)
V. Whoop, _____, Sloop!
W. They tried to keep the men off of the train
X. It held Bud's blanket, flyer & things
Y. Instrument band gave to Bud

Bud, Not Buddy Matching 2

___ 1. MOMMA A. Cardboard town for the homeless
___ 2. TELEGRAM B. Guards at the shed door
___ 3. TEARS C. Momma ___ to Bud until he fell asleep
___ 4. GRACE D. J. Edgar ____; head of FBI for 48 years
___ 5. HOOVER E. Lefty sent one to HEC, advising him of Bud's whereabouts
___ 6. SHED F. Steady ____
___ 7. HOME G. ____ Hoover; President of United States
___ 8. FISH H. Mr. Lewis
___ 9. JERRY I. Ku Klux ____; organization against equal rights; members anonymous
___10. CALDWELL J. Bud's pretend name at the mission
___11. MICHIGAN K. Bud's last name
___12. EDDIE L. She was unhappy at the Miss B. Gotten Moon Park
___13. DOOR M. He got a foster home with girls
___14. HERBERT N. Lefty was transporting this, so Bud thought he was a vampire
___15. HORNETS O. Bud's had all dried up; he didn't cry often
___16. HOOVERVILLE P. The vampire bat was actually this kind of a nest
___17. RULES Q. John ____; abolitionist
___18. SAXOPHONE R. Bud's word for the orphanage
___19. BLOOD S. Mr. ___ locked Bud in the shed
___20. KLAN T. Instrument band gave to Bud
___21. BROWN U. When one closes, another one opens
___22. READ V. _____ & Things Number 328
___23. CLARENCE W. Miss Thomas's first name
___24. LEFTY X. Where Amoses locked Bud
___25. AMOS Y. State where Bud lived

Bud, Not Buddy Matching 2 Answer Key

L - 1. MOMMA	A.	Cardboard town for the homeless
E - 2. TELEGRAM	B.	Guards at the shed door
O - 3. TEARS	C.	Momma ___ to Bud until he fell asleep
W - 4. GRACE	D.	J. Edgar ____; head of FBI for 48 years
D - 5. HOOVER	E.	Lefty sent one to HEC, advising him of Bud's whereabouts
X - 6. SHED	F.	Steady ____
R - 7. HOME	G.	____ Hoover; President of United States
B - 8. FISH	H.	Mr. Lewis
M - 9. JERRY	I.	Ku Klux ____; organization against equal rights; members anonymous
K - 10. CALDWELL	J.	Bud's pretend name at the mission
Y - 11. MICHIGAN	K.	Bud's last name
F - 12. EDDIE	L.	She was unhappy at the Miss B. Gotten Moon Park
U - 13. DOOR	M.	He got a foster home with girls
G - 14. HERBERT	N.	Lefty was transporting this, so Bud thought he was a vampire
P - 15. HORNETS	O.	Bud's had all dried up; he didn't cry often
A - 16. HOOVERVILLE	P.	The vampire bat was actually this kind of a nest
V - 17. RULES	Q.	John ____; abolitionist
T - 18. SAXOPHONE	R.	Bud's word for the orphanage
N - 19. BLOOD	S.	Mr. ___ locked Bud in the shed
I - 20. KLAN	T.	Instrument band gave to Bud
Q - 21. BROWN	U.	When one closes, another one opens
C - 22. READ	V.	____ & Things Number 328
J - 23. CLARENCE	W.	Miss Thomas's first name
H - 24. LEFTY	X.	Where Amoses locked Bud
S - 25. AMOS	Y.	State where Bud lived

Bud, Not Buddy Matching 3

___ 1. RULES A. Mr. Lewis
___ 2. STATION B. Instrument band gave to Bud
___ 3. SUITCASE C. HEC's instrument; a giant ____
___ 4. BUD D. They tried to keep the men off of the train
___ 5. FBI E. When one closes, another one opens
___ 6. CAR F. ____, Not Buddy
___ 7. DOOR G. Grand ____; where HEC lived
___ 8. JERRY H. Mrs. ___ was Lefty's daughter
___ 9. SAXOPHONE I. Machine Gun ____; gangster
___ 10. CALDWELL J. ____ Hoover; President of United States
___ 11. AMOS K. Grand Calloway ____
___ 12. FIDDLE L. Miss ___; vocal stylist who took care of Bud
___ 13. STONES M. Miss Malone
___ 14. TELEGRAM N. Lefty sent one to HEC, advising him of Bud's whereabouts
___ 15. FLYERS O. Had numbers & letters written on them
___ 16. PEA P. He got a foster home with girls
___ 17. RAPIDS Q. ____ & Things Number 328
___ 18. COPS R. Bud's last name
___ 19. THOMAS S. Bud tried to drive Lefty's away
___ 20. JIMMY T. Horn player who helped Bud
___ 21. HERBERT U. It held Bud's blanket, flyer & things
___ 22. DEZA V. Mr. ___ locked Bud in the shed
___ 23. SLEET W. They had printed information about HEC and the band
___ 24. KELLY X. Federal Bureau of Investigation
___ 25. LEFTY Y. Sweet ___; restaurant

Bud, Not Buddy Matching 3 Answer Key

Q - 1. RULES		A. Mr. Lewis
K - 2. STATION		B. Instrument band gave to Bud
U - 3. SUITCASE		C. HEC's instrument; a giant ____
F - 4. BUD		D. They tried to keep the men off of the train
X - 5. FBI		E. When one closes, another one opens
S - 6. CAR		F. ____, Not Buddy
E - 7. DOOR		G. Grand ____; where HEC lived
P - 8. JERRY		H. Mrs. ___ was Lefty's daughter
B - 9. SAXOPHONE		I. Machine Gun ____; gangster
R -10. CALDWELL		J. ____ Hoover; President of United States
V -11. AMOS		K. Grand Calloway _____
C -12. FIDDLE		L. Miss ___; vocal stylist who took care of Bud
O -13. STONES		M. Miss Malone
N -14. TELEGRAM		N. Lefty sent one to HEC, advising him of Bud's whereabouts
W -15. FLYERS		O. Had numbers & letters written on them
Y -16. PEA		P. He got a foster home with girls
G -17. RAPIDS		Q. _____ & Things Number 328
D -18. COPS		R. Bud's last name
L - 19. THOMAS		S. Bud tried to drive Lefty's away
T - 20. JIMMY		T. Horn player who helped Bud
J - 21. HERBERT		U. It held Bud's blanket, flyer & things
M -22. DEZA		V. Mr. ___ locked Bud in the shed
H -23. SLEET		W. They had printed information about HEC and the band
I - 24. KELLY		X. Federal Bureau of Investigation
A -25. LEFTY		Y. Sweet ___; restaurant

Copyrighted

Bud, Not Buddy Matching 4

___ 1. ZOOP   A. Bud's word for the orphanage
___ 2. GRACE   B. J. Edgar ____; head of FBI for 48 years
___ 3. RAPIDS   C. The boys wanted to hop on one going west
___ 4. STONES   D. Gone = ____ (Rule 28)
___ 5. PEA   E. City where Bud & Momma lived
___ 6. FLINT   F. Bud's last name
___ 7. SHED   G. Bud looked for Miss Hill there
___ 8. LEFTY   H. Whoop, _____, Sloop!
___ 9. DEAD   I. Police stopped Lefty looking for ___ organizers
___10. HOOVER   J. ___ caps; men who handled baggage at the train
___11. SLEEPY   K. Where Amoses locked Bud
___12. LIBRARY   L. Sweet ___; restaurant
___13. HORNETS   M. On the ___; running away
___14. DOOR   N. Steady ____
___15. CALDWELL   O. Miss Thomas's first name
___16. RED   P. The vampire bat was actually this kind of a nest
___17. LABOR   Q. Mr. Lewis
___18. MICHIGAN   R. When one closes, another one opens
___19. EDDIE   S. 1st part of the revenge plan was to get rid of this
___20. GUN   T. Had numbers & letters written on them
___21. FIDDLE   U. HEC's instrument; a giant ____
___22. LAM   V. John ____; abolitionist
___23. BROWN   W. State where Bud lived
___24. HOME   X. ___ LaBone; Bud
___25. TRAIN   Y. Grand ____; where HEC lived

Bud, Not Buddy Matching 4 Answer Key

H - 1. ZOOP	A.	Bud's word for the orphanage
O - 2. GRACE	B.	J. Edgar ____; head of FBI for 48 years
Y - 3. RAPIDS	C.	The boys wanted to hop on one going west
T - 4. STONES	D.	Gone = ____ (Rule 28)
L - 5. PEA	E.	City where Bud & Momma lived
E - 6. FLINT	F.	Bud's last name
K - 7. SHED	G.	Bud looked for Miss Hill there
Q - 8. LEFTY	H.	Whoop, _____, Sloop!
D - 9. DEAD	I.	Police stopped Lefty looking for ___ organizers
B - 10. HOOVER	J.	___ caps; men who handled baggage at the train
X - 11. SLEEPY	K.	Where Amoses locked Bud
G - 12. LIBRARY	L.	Sweet ___; restaurant
P - 13. HORNETS	M.	On the ___; running away
R - 14. DOOR	N.	Steady ____
F - 15. CALDWELL	O.	Miss Thomas's first name
J - 16. RED	P.	The vampire bat was actually this kind of a nest
I - 17. LABOR	Q.	Mr. Lewis
W - 18. MICHIGAN	R.	When one closes, another one opens
N - 19. EDDIE	S.	1st part of the revenge plan was to get rid of this
S - 20. GUN	T.	Had numbers & letters written on them
U - 21. FIDDLE	U.	HEC's instrument; a giant ____
M - 22. LAM	V.	John ____; abolitionist
V - 23. BROWN	W.	State where Bud lived
A - 24. HOME	X.	___ LaBone; Bud
C - 25. TRAIN	Y.	Grand ____; where HEC lived

Bud, Not Buddy Magic Squares 1

Match the definition with the vocabulary word. Put your answers in the magic squares below. When your answers are correct, all columns and rows will add to the same number.

A. HOOVERVILLE
B. EDDIE
C. KLAN
D. PEA
E. CAPONE
F. HOOVER
G. SHED
H. TELEGRAM
I. ZOOP
J. FISH
K. RED
L. SAXOPHONE
M. LABOR
N. SLEEPY
O. MOMMA
P. THOMAS

1. Steady ____
2. Where Amoses locked Bud
3. ____ caps; men who handled baggage at the train
4. ____ LaBone; Bud
5. Police stopped Lefty looking for ____ organizers
6. Instrument band gave to Bud
7. Lefty sent one to HEC, advising him of Bud's whereabouts
8. Cardboard town for the homeless
9. Miss ____; vocal stylist who took care of Bud
10. Whoop, ____, Sloop!
11. Al ____; leader of Chicago underworld
12. Sweet ____; restaurant
13. Ku Klux ____; organization against equal rights; members anonymous
14. J. Edgar ____; head of FBI for 48 years
15. Guards at the shed door
16. She was unhappy at the Miss B. Gotten Moon Park

A=	B=	C=	D=
E=	F=	G=	H=
I=	J=	K=	L=
M=	N=	O=	P=

Bud, Not Buddy Magic Squares 1 Answer Key

Match the definition with the vocabulary word. Put your answers in the magic squares below. When your answers are correct, all columns and rows will add to the same number.

A. HOOVERVILLE
B. EDDIE
C. KLAN
D. PEA
E. CAPONE
F. HOOVER
G. SHED
H. TELEGRAM
I. ZOOP
J. FISH
K. RED
L. SAXOPHONE
M. LABOR
N. SLEEPY
O. MOMMA
P. THOMAS

1. Steady ____
2. Where Amoses locked Bud
3. ___ caps; men who handled baggage at the train
4. ___ LaBone; Bud
5. Police stopped Lefty looking for ___ organizers
6. Instrument band gave to Bud
7. Lefty sent one to HEC, advising him of Bud's whereabouts
8. Cardboard town for the homeless
9. Miss ___; vocal stylist who took care of Bud
10. Whoop, _____, Sloop!
11. Al ____; leader of Chicago underworld
12. Sweet ___; restaurant
13. Ku Klux ____; organization against equal rights; members anonymous
14. J. Edgar ____; head of FBI for 48 years
15. Guards at the shed door
16. She was unhappy at the Miss B. Gotten Moon Park

A=8	B=1	C=13	D=12
E=11	F=14	G=2	H=7
I=10	J=15	K=3	L=6
M=5	N=4	O=16	P=9

Bud, Not Buddy Magic Squares 2

Match the definition with the vocabulary word. Put your answers in the magic squares below. When your answers are correct, all columns and rows will add to the same number.

A. SEEDS
B. HOME
C. SAXOPHONE
D. THOMAS
E. HOOVERVILLE
F. KELLY
G. STATION
H. DEZA
I. HORNETS
J. SLEET
K. SUITCASE
L. FBI
M. HOOVER
N. BROWN
O. GUN
P. MOMMA

1. Ideas are a lot like these
2. John ____; abolitionist
3. Mrs. ___ was Lefty's daughter
4. Cardboard town for the homeless
5. Grand Calloway _____
6. Federal Bureau of Investigation
7. She was unhappy at the Miss B. Gotten Moon Park
8. Instrument band gave to Bud
9. 1st part of the revenge plan was to get rid of this
10. Miss ___; vocal stylist who took care of Bud
11. Miss Malone
12. It held Bud's blanket, flyer & things
13. The vampire bat was actually this kind of a nest
14. Machine Gun ____; gangster
15. Bud's word for the orphanage
16. J. Edgar ____; head of FBI for 48 years

A=	B=	C=	D=
E=	F=	G=	H=
I=	J=	K=	L=
M=	N=	O=	P=

Bud, Not Buddy Magic Squares 2 Answer Key

Match the definition with the vocabulary word. Put your answers in the magic squares below. When your answers are correct, all columns and rows will add to the same number.

A. SEEDS
B. HOME
C. SAXOPHONE
D. THOMAS
E. HOOVERVILLE
F. KELLY
G. STATION
H. DEZA
I. HORNETS
J. SLEET
K. SUITCASE
L. FBI
M. HOOVER
N. BROWN
O. GUN
P. MOMMA

1. Ideas are a lot like these
2. John ____; abolitionist
3. Mrs. ___ was Lefty's daughter
4. Cardboard town for the homeless
5. Grand Calloway _____
6. Federal Bureau of Investigation
7. She was unhappy at the Miss B. Gotten Moon Park
8. Instrument band gave to Bud
9. 1st part of the revenge plan was to get rid of this
10. Miss ___; vocal stylist who took care of Bud
11. Miss Malone
12. It held Bud's blanket, flyer & things
13. The vampire bat was actually this kind of a nest
14. Machine Gun ____; gangster
15. Bud's word for the orphanage
16. J. Edgar ____; head of FBI for 48 years

A=1	B=15	C=8	D=10
E=4	F=14	G=5	H=11
I=13	J=3	K=12	L=6
M=16	N=2	O=9	P=7

Bud, Not Buddy Magic Squares 3

Match the definition with the vocabulary word. Put your answers in the magic squares below. When your answers are correct, all columns and rows will add to the same number.

A. CAR
B. CLARENCE
C. DEZA
D. GUN
E. DOOR
F. SEEDS
G. SLEEPY
H. FISH
I. EDDIE
J. STONES
K. DEAD
L. HORNETS
M. CALLOWAY
N. MISSION
O. HERMAN
P. PEA

1. Herman E. _____
2. Ideas are a lot like these
3. Guards at the shed door
4. Mr. Calloway's first name
5. The vampire bat was actually this kind of a nest
6. Miss Malone
7. Bud tried to drive Lefty's away
8. Had numbers & letters written on them
9. Gone = ____ (Rule 28)
10. 1st part of the revenge plan was to get rid of this
11. Bud's pretend name at the mission
12. Steady ____
13. Place where Bud got food
14. When one closes, another one opens
15. ___ LaBone; Bud
16. Sweet ___; restaurant

A=	B=	C=	D=
E=	F=	G=	H=
I=	J=	K=	L=
M=	N=	O=	P=

Bud, Not Buddy Magic Squares 3 Answer Key

Match the definition with the vocabulary word. Put your answers in the magic squares below. When your answers are correct, all columns and rows will add to the same number.

A. CAR
B. CLARENCE
C. DEZA
D. GUN
E. DOOR
F. SEEDS
G. SLEEPY
H. FISH
I. EDDIE
J. STONES
K. DEAD
L. HORNETS
M. CALLOWAY
N. MISSION
O. HERMAN
P. PEA

1. Herman E. _____
2. Ideas are a lot like these
3. Guards at the shed door
4. Mr. Calloway's first name
5. The vampire bat was actually this kind of a nest
6. Miss Malone
7. Bud tried to drive Lefty's away
8. Had numbers & letters written on them
9. Gone = _____ (Rule 28)
10. 1st part of the revenge plan was to get rid of this
11. Bud's pretend name at the mission
12. Steady _____
13. Place where Bud got food
14. When one closes, another one opens
15. ___ LaBone; Bud
16. Sweet ___; restaurant

A=7	B=11	C=6	D=10
E=14	F=2	G=15	H=3
I=12	J=8	K=9	L=5
M=1	N=13	O=4	P=16

Bud, Not Buddy Magic Squares 4

Match the definition with the vocabulary word. Put your answers in the magic squares below. When your answers are correct, all columns and rows will add to the same number.

A. GUN
B. RED
C. HERMAN
D. SUITCASE
E. MOMMA
F. EDDIE
G. MISSION
H. SAXOPHONE
I. HOOVER
J. FIDDLE
K. FLINT
L. GRACE
M. DEPRESSION
N. LEFTY
O. CALDWELL
P. HOME

1. Instrument band gave to Bud
2. 1st part of the revenge plan was to get rid of this
3. ___ caps; men who handled baggage at the train
4. Place where Bud got food
5. HEC's instrument; a giant ____
6. Bud's last name
7. Bud's word for the orphanage
8. J. Edgar ____; head of FBI for 48 years
9. City where Bud & Momma lived
10. Mr. Lewis
11. HEC & The Dusky Devastators of the _____
12. Miss Thomas's first name
13. She was unhappy at the Miss B. Gotten Moon Park
14. It held Bud's blanket, flyer & things
15. Mr. Calloway's first name
16. Steady ____

A=	B=	C=	D=
E=	F=	G=	H=
I=	J=	K=	L=
M=	N=	O=	P=

Copyrighted

Bud, Not Buddy Magic Squares 4 Answer Key

Match the definition with the vocabulary word. Put your answers in the magic squares below. When your answers are correct, all columns and rows will add to the same number.

A. GUN
B. RED
C. HERMAN
D. SUITCASE
E. MOMMA
F. EDDIE
G. MISSION
H. SAXOPHONE
I. HOOVER
J. FIDDLE
K. FLINT
L. GRACE
M. DEPRESSION
N. LEFTY
O. CALDWELL
P. HOME

1. Instrument band gave to Bud
2. 1st part of the revenge plan was to get rid of this
3. ___ caps; men who handled baggage at the train
4. Place where Bud got food
5. HEC's instrument; a giant ____
6. Bud's last name
7. Bud's word for the orphanage
8. J. Edgar ____; head of FBI for 48 years
9. City where Bud & Momma lived
10. Mr. Lewis
11. HEC & The Dusky Devastators of the _____
12. Miss Thomas's first name
13. She was unhappy at the Miss B. Gotten Moon Park
14. It held Bud's blanket, flyer & things
15. Mr. Calloway's first name
16. Steady ____

A=2	B=3	C=15	D=14
E=13	F=16	G=4	H=1
I=8	J=5	K=9	L=12
M=11	N=10	O=6	P=7

Bud, Not Buddy Word Search 1

```
Q L A M H E R B E R T D T V N T F B
G U N H N O I S S I M D O O R H L Q
S P G D B H O E Z R G U L A A O Y R
H M E A K J N V U V T B I N C R E S
E I L Y D O V L E Z H N W B R N R L
D C A H T E E L S R Z O O P E E S X
M H S S E S A G T Q R R M I A T A H
Y I G G A B U D A B Z C D E D S M N
F G H K R B L F T F A D Y J Z Z O R
P A Q T S E B O I P E A M M O M H B
G N M C G S D B O D J Z M O Q L T T
X R N O H A F N N D D X I C O H S T
P E A J S C E Y T F E L J O X N D X
Y Y L C Y T N I L F Z F E P M N I W
T J K K E I T E K N A L B S N L P Q
S E E D S U C A L D W E L L B G A C
Y P E E L S G R A N D F A T H E R R
```

1st part of the revenge plan was to get rid of this (3)
A cockroach crawled in his ear (4)
Al ____; leader of Chicago underworld (6)
Bud tried to drive Lefty's away (3)
Bud's had all dried up; he didn't cry often (5)
Bud's last name (8)
Bud's word for the orphanage (4)
City where Bud & Momma lived (5)
Federal Bureau of Investigation (3)
Gone = ____ (Rule 28) (4)
Grand Calloway ____ (7)
Grand ____; where HEC lived (6)
Guards at the shed door (4)
HEC to Bud (11)
HEC's instrument; a giant ____ (6)
Had numbers & letters written on them (6)
Horn player who helped Bud (5)
Ideas are a lot like these (5)
It held Bud's blanket, flyer & things (8)
J. Edgar ____; head of FBI for 48 years (6)
John ____; abolitionist (5)
Ku Klux ____; organization against equal rights; members anonymous (4)
Lefty was transporting this, so Bud thought he was a vampire (5)
Miss B. Gotten ____ Park (4)
Miss Malone (4)
Miss Thomas's first name (5)
Miss ___; vocal stylist who took care of Bud (6)
Momma ___ to Bud until he fell asleep (4)

Mr. Lewis (5)
Mr. ___ locked Bud in the shed (4)
Mrs. ___ was Lefty's daughter (5)
On the ___; running away (3)
Place where Bud got food (7)
Police stopped Lefty looking for ___ organizers (5)
She was unhappy at the Miss B. Gotten Moon Park (5)
State where Bud lived (8)
Steady ____ (5)
Sweet ___; restaurant (3)
The boys wanted to hop on one going west (5)
The vampire bat was actually this kind of a nest (7)
They had printed information about HEC and the band (6)
They tried to keep the men off of the train (4)
When one closes, another one opens (4)
When wrapped in it, Bud felt close to Momma (7)
Where Amoses locked Bud (4)
Whoop, ____, Sloop! (4)
____ LaBone; Bud (6)
___ caps; men who handled baggage at the train (3)
____ Hoover; President of United States (7)
____ Janet; Momma (6)
____, Not Buddy (3)
____ & Things Number 328 (5)

Bud, Not Buddy Word Search 1 Answer Key

```
      L  A  M  H  E  R  B  E  R  T              T  F
   G  U        N  O  I  S  S  I  M     D  O  O  R  H  L
   S           N     O  E     R        U     A     O  Y
   H  M  E     A     N  V  U           B  I  N     C  E
   E  I  L     D  O     L  E        H  N  W     R  N  R
   D  C  A  H  T  E  E  L  S  R  Z  O  O  P     E  E  S
      H  S  S  E  A  G  T        R     M  I  A  D  T  A
               A  B  U  D  A  B     C  D  E  D     S  M
   F        G  R  B  L  F  T     A  D  Y              O
            A  S  E     O  I  P  E  A  M  M  O  M     H
   G  N  M        S  D  B  O  D     M  O           T
      R  N  O     A  F  N  N  D     I  C     O        S
   P  E  A        S  C  E  Y  T  F  E  L  J  O     N  D
         L        C  T  N  I  L  F  Z     E  P        I
         K        E  I  T  E  K  N  A  L  B  S        P
   S  E  E  D  S  U  C  A  L  D  W  E  L  L           A
   Y  P  E  E  L  S  G  R  A  N  D  F  A  T  H  E  R
```

1st part of the revenge plan was to get rid of this (3)
A cockroach crawled in his ear (4)
Al ____; leader of Chicago underworld (6)
Bud tried to drive Lefty's away (3)
Bud's had all dried up; he didn't cry often (5)
Bud's last name (8)
Bud's word for the orphanage (4)
City where Bud & Momma lived (5)
Federal Bureau of Investigation (3)
Gone = ____ (Rule 28) (4)
Grand Calloway ____ (7)
Grand ____; where HEC lived (6)
Guards at the shed door (4)
HEC to Bud (11)
HEC's instrument; a giant ____ (6)
Had numbers & letters written on them (6)
Horn player who helped Bud (5)
Ideas are a lot like these (5)
It held Bud's blanket, flyer & things (8)
J. Edgar ____; head of FBI for 48 years (6)
John ____; abolitionist (5)
Ku Klux ____; organization against equal rights; members anonymous (4)
Lefty was transporting this, so Bud thought he was a vampire (5)
Miss B. Gotten ____ Park (4)
Miss Malone (4)
Miss Thomas's first name (5)
Miss ___; vocal stylist who took care of Bud (6)
Momma ___ to Bud until he fell asleep (4)
Mr. Lewis (5)
Mr. ___ locked Bud in the shed (4)
Mrs. ___ was Lefty's daughter (5)
On the ___; running away (3)
Place where Bud got food (7)
Police stopped Lefty looking for ___ organizers (5)
She was unhappy at the Miss B. Gotten Moon Park (5)
State where Bud lived (8)
Steady ____ (5)
Sweet ___; restaurant (3)
The boys wanted to hop on one going west (5)
The vampire bat was actually this kind of a nest (7)
They had printed information about HEC and the band (6)
They tried to keep the men off of the train (4)
When one closes, another one opens (4)
When wrapped in it, Bud felt close to Momma (7)
Where Amoses locked Bud (4)
Whoop, _____, Sloop! (4)
___ LaBone; Bud (6)
___ caps; men who handled baggage at the train (3)
____ Hoover; President of United States (7)
____ Janet; Momma (6)
____, Not Buddy (3)
_____ & Things Number 328 (5)

Bud, Not Buddy Word Search 2

```
F L I B R A R Y R R E J F S D H S H
I R T W T N S O A U Z Y R S L E E T
S Y P Z N T B N P J L A J S E R A J
H P K Z I A Y N I D E E A D Z M N D
B J N C L J O Y D T S X S P A A P V
B R I L F I H X S X O U R L H N H L
L G A Y T F E L C P N O I S S I M M
A N R A N A G I H C I M Z T K L D R
N N T A H N H O S L K G O M C Q E T
K S Q S C G N H T D L F O A Q A H J
E R H O M E T H O M A S P B U G S Q
T B D H D L G O N R N O J H Y O R E
B K M O B A L B E G N P W R M R E T
Q R S C O B P U S E U E Q A M E Y B
H O O V E R E D M O O N T I A L T
N P W W A X A K E L L Y B S J D F J
S B L C N D E Z A B N F M O M M A C
```

1st part of the revenge plan was to get rid of this (3)
A cockroach crawled in his ear (4)
Al ____; leader of Chicago underworld (6)
Bud looked for Miss Hill there (7)
Bud tried to drive Lefty's away (3)
Bud's had all dried up; he didn't cry often (5)
Bud's word for the orphanage (4)
City where Bud & Momma lived (5)
Federal Bureau of Investigation (3)
Gone = ____ (Rule 28) (4)
Grand Calloway _____ (7)
Grand ____; where HEC lived (6)
Guards at the shed door (4)
Had numbers & letters written on them (6)
He got a foster home with girls (5)
Horn player who helped Bud (5)
Ideas are a lot like these (5)
Instrument band gave to Bud (9)
It held Bud's blanket, flyer & things (8)
J. Edgar ____; head of FBI for 48 years (6)
John ____; abolitionist (5)
Ku Klux ____; organization against equal rights; members anonymous (4)
Lefty was transporting this, so Bud thought he was a vampire (5)
Machine Gun ____; gangster (5)
Miss B. Gotten ____ Park (4)
Miss Malone (4)
Miss Thomas's first name (5)
Miss ___; vocal stylist who took care of Bud (6)

Momma ___ to Bud until he fell asleep (4)
Mr. Calloway's first name (6)
Mr. Lewis (5)
Mr. ___ locked Bud in the shed (4)
Mrs. ___ was Lefty's daughter (5)
On the ___; running away (3)
Place where Bud got food (7)
Police stopped Lefty looking for ___ organizers (5)
She was unhappy at the Miss B. Gotten Moon Park (5)
State where Bud lived (8)
Sweet ___; restaurant (3)
The boys wanted to hop on one going west (5)
The vampire bat was actually this kind of a nest (7)
They had printed information about HEC and the band (6)
They tried to keep the men off of the train (4)
When one closes, another one opens (4)
When wrapped in it, Bud felt close to Momma (7)
Where Amoses locked Bud (4)
Whoop, _____, Sloop! (4)
___ caps; men who handled baggage at the train (3)
____ Janet; Momma (6)
____, Not Buddy (3)
_____ & Things Number 328 (5)

Bud, Not Buddy Word Search 2 Answer Key

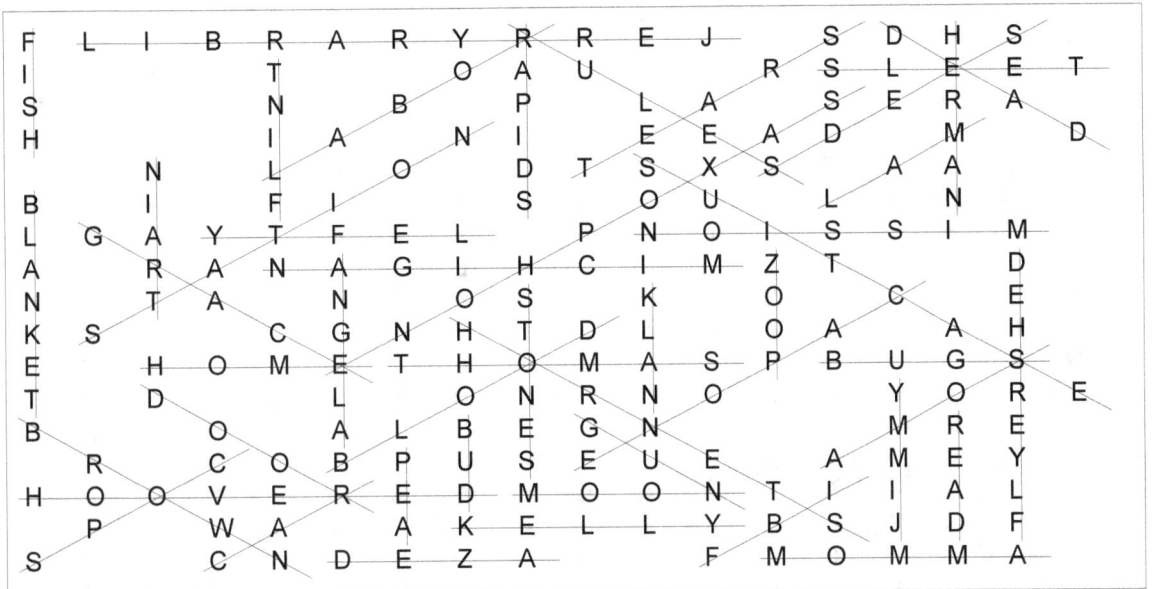

1st part of the revenge plan was to get rid of this (3)
A cockroach crawled in his ear (4)
Al ____; leader of Chicago underworld (6)
Bud looked for Miss Hill there (7)
Bud tried to drive Lefty's away (3)
Bud's had all dried up; he didn't cry often (5)
Bud's word for the orphanage (4)
City where Bud & Momma lived (5)
Federal Bureau of Investigation (3)
Gone = ____ (Rule 28) (4)
Grand Calloway ____ (7)
Grand ____; where HEC lived (6)
Guards at the shed door (4)
Had numbers & letters written on them (6)
He got a foster home with girls (5)
Horn player who helped Bud (5)
Ideas are a lot like these (5)
Instrument band gave to Bud (9)
It held Bud's blanket, flyer & things (8)
J. Edgar ____; head of FBI for 48 years (6)
John ____; abolitionist (5)
Ku Klux ____; organization against equal rights; members anonymous (4)
Lefty was transporting this, so Bud thought he was a vampire (5)
Machine Gun ____; gangster (5)
Miss B. Gotten ____ Park (4)
Miss Malone (4)
Miss Thomas's first name (5)
Miss ____; vocal stylist who took care of Bud (6)

Momma ___ to Bud until he fell asleep (4)
Mr. Calloway's first name (6)
Mr. Lewis (5)
Mr. ___ locked Bud in the shed (4)
Mrs. ___ was Lefty's daughter (5)
On the ___; running away (3)
Place where Bud got food (7)
Police stopped Lefty looking for ___ organizers (5)
She was unhappy at the Miss B. Gotten Moon Park (5)
State where Bud lived (8)
Sweet ___; restaurant (3)
The boys wanted to hop on one going west (5)
The vampire bat was actually this kind of a nest (7)
They had printed information about HEC and the band (6)
They tried to keep the men off of the train (4)
When one closes, another one opens (4)
When wrapped in it, Bud felt close to Momma (7)
Where Amoses locked Bud (4)
Whoop, _____, Sloop! (4)
___ caps; men who handled baggage at the train (3)
____ Janet; Momma (6)
____, Not Buddy (3)
_____ & Things Number 328 (5)

Bud, Not Buddy Word Search 3

```
B L O O D N N S T E N R O H E S T T
J U S Y K O P L T E U D C C L N T V
I R G P I O Z C G O N A A I B R Z
M H E S C B F A X H N B L B Y A H
M S S D I P A R S P R F D R H N Y
Y I O E J J V I M X E S B W A M P
M O F M E H F H O M S N B E R C N
R J I K H D L B M A K E L L Y A O
F Y D L R N S C M R O B A L D P I
B N D J T W B R A G S Z A N Q O T
X H L E R N S N U E K L Z N G N A
T R E B R E H U C L A R E N C E T
F L F R L O T P I E E I D E A F S
S L T F M A M L D D S B R P V L
H C Y E B N R A D C F S U H Y J E
M O O N Z I N K E N F A L K D P R
B R O Y W N O Z Z E A V M S Y G E R
X P Y V R P O R S T D L E E A R Y
D E A D E D E P R E S S I O N R S
S H E D G R A N D F A T H E R S R
```

AMOS	FISH	MISSION
ANGELA	FLINT	MOMMA
BLANKET	FLYERS	MOON
BLOOD	GRACE	PEA
BROWN	GRANDFATHER	RAPIDS
BUD	GUN	READ
BUGS	HERBERT	RED
CALDWELL	HERMAN	RULES
CAPONE	HOME	SEEDS
CAR	HOOVER	SHED
CLARENCE	HORNETS	SLEEPY
COPS	JERRY	SLEET
DEAD	JIMMY	STATION
DEPRESSION	KELLY	STONES
DEZA	KLAN	SUITCASE
DOOR	LABOR	TEARS
EDDIE	LAM	TELEGRAM
FBI	LEFTY	TRAIN
FIDDLE	LIBRARY	ZOOP

Bud, Not Buddy Word Search 3 Answer Key

```
B L O O D   N S T E N R O H E   T
J U       O P T U   C   N   R
I R   G I O C G O   A   L   A
M E S C   A H N R   L B   I
M S D I P A R S   G E F D W   N
Y I O E     F     M     S W E   O
  M O F   E D     O M A K   E R C
  R F     S M R G S L L Y A
      I     R A E L A   P
      D   T S U C   Z   O
    H E B R E H U C L A R E N C E
  T R L F L O     I E D B   P   S
    L T F M     L T C S U   Y   L
  S   Y E B A N R A D C F K P E A
  H   E N Z I N K E M N A L D A R
  M   O O W N O   E A   M S Y E R
  B R O W N V       T D O   E E R
      D E A D E D E P R E S S I O N S
    S H E D G R A N D F A T H E R
```

AMOS	FISH	MISSION
ANGELA	FLINT	MOMMA
BLANKET	FLYERS	MOON
BLOOD	GRACE	PEA
BROWN	GRANDFATHER	RAPIDS
BUD	GUN	READ
BUGS	HERBERT	RED
CALDWELL	HERMAN	RULES
CAPONE	HOME	SEEDS
CAR	HOOVER	SHED
CLARENCE	HORNETS	SLEEPY
COPS	JERRY	SLEET
DEAD	JIMMY	STATION
DEPRESSION	KELLY	STONES
DEZA	KLAN	SUITCASE
DOOR	LABOR	TEARS
EDDIE	LAM	TELEGRAM
FBI	LEFTY	TRAIN
FIDDLE	LIBRARY	ZOOP

Bud, Not Buddy Word Search 4

```
F L Y E R S J H S I F S A M O H T H
H I R P Y C E O N T D L Y G R M W
E G D Z P L R M L I E R J E A X O D
R U V D S A R E P G B U S I V O Z
B N T P L R Y A N Z L N S M P N M
E X O G E E R A Y S G E T C M Y T
R C T V X N B M D C S T A A P Y M
T K O T M C W B G C E I P F Z S
N O I S S E R P E D E E N H I O N D F
H B M A R G E L E T N C O O N M T V
N Y A W O L L A C Z S R I N M E L H
V D N K V E M E W M Y O M G K H V S
W D H W W M Q D N V R H T N I L F H
M E S D R T C D L Y A W A Z G D N L
M Z L D P D A I T A R L O M U I G
N A M R E H R R E A D B L O D F T L W
C G M H A A A C Z D I O M R F T L K
B H S O W R D A O F L M R N L L Y
D O O R S P P R O N A E L S B A E W
S T O N E S R G P T E E L S D M K V
```

AMOS
ANGELA
BLANKET
BLOOD
BROWN
BUD
BUGS
CALDWELL
CALLOWAY
CAPONE
CAR
CLARENCE
COPS
DEAD
DEPRESSION

DEZA
DOOR
EDDIE
FBI
FIDDLE
FISH
FLINT
FLYERS
GRACE
GUN
HERBERT
HERMAN
HOME
HOOVER
HORNETS

JERRY
JIMMY
KELLY
KLAN
LABOR
LAM
LEFTY
LIBRARY
MICHIGAN
MOMMA
MOON
PEA
RAPIDS
READ
RED

RULES
SEEDS
SHED
SLEEPY
SLEET
STATION
STONES
TEARS
TELEGRAM
THOMAS
TRAIN
ZOOP

Bud, Not Buddy Word Search 4 Answer Key

AMOS	DEZA	JERRY	RULES
ANGELA	DOOR	JIMMY	SEEDS
BLANKET	EDDIE	KELLY	SHED
BLOOD	FBI	KLAN	SLEEPY
BROWN	FIDDLE	LABOR	SLEET
BUD	FISH	LAM	STATION
BUGS	FLINT	LEFTY	STONES
CALDWELL	FLYERS	LIBRARY	TEARS
CALLOWAY	GRACE	MICHIGAN	TELEGRAM
CAPONE	GUN	MOMMA	THOMAS
CAR	HERBERT	MOON	TRAIN
CLARENCE	HERMAN	PEA	ZOOP
COPS	HOME	RAPIDS	
DEAD	HOOVER	READ	
DEPRESSION	HORNETS	RED	

Bud, Not Buddy Crossword 1

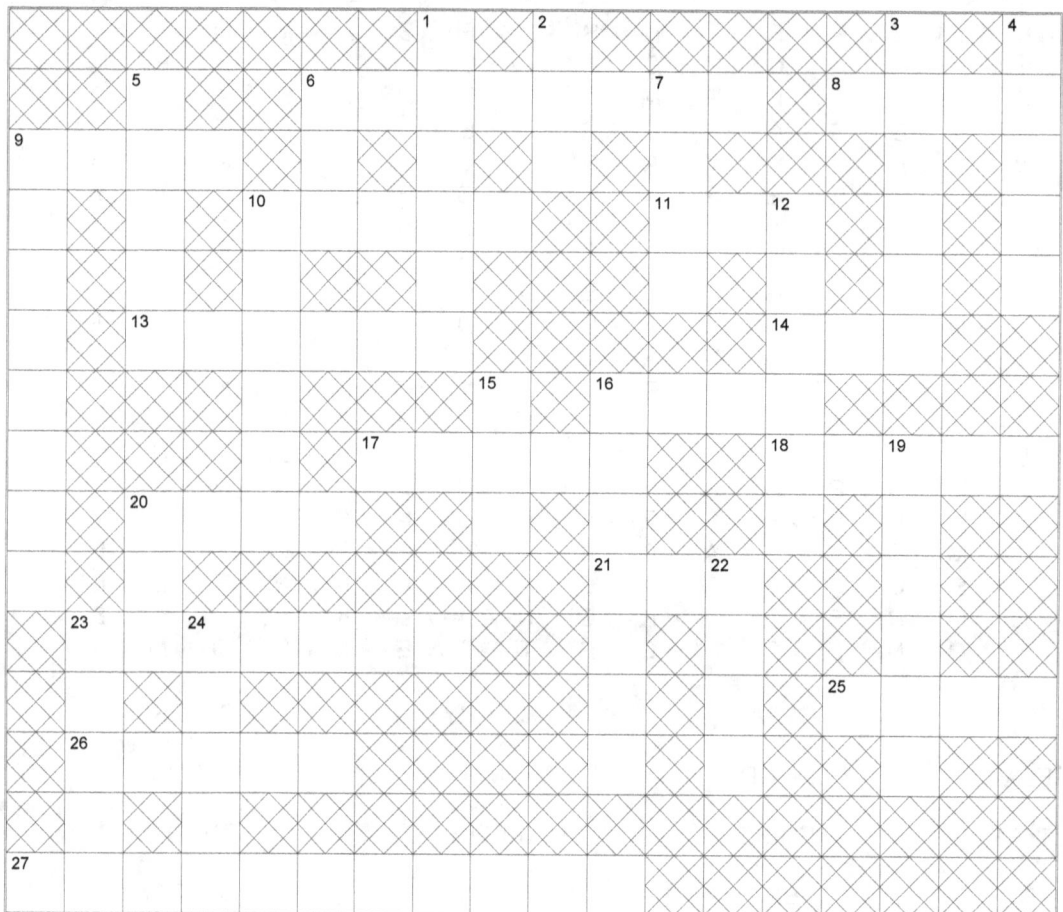

Across
6. Bud's pretend name at the mission
8. Momma ___ to Bud until he fell asleep
9. Where Amoses locked Bud
10. The boys wanted to hop on one going west
11. Sweet ___; restaurant
13. Had numbers & letters written on them
14. 1st part of the revenge plan was to get rid of this
16. Bud's word for the orphanage
17. Miss Thomas's first name
18. Mr. Lewis
20. Guards at the shed door
21. ___, Not Buddy
23. Bud looked for Miss Hill there
25. Ku Klux ___; organization against equal rights; members anonymous
26. Lefty was transporting this, so Bud thought he was a vampire
27. HEC to Bud

Down
1. Grand ___; where HEC lived
2. ___ caps; men who handled baggage at the train
3. Mr. Calloway's first name
4. Steady ___
5. Ideas are a lot like these
6. Bud tried to drive Lefty's away
7. They tried to keep the men off of the train
9. It held Bud's blanket, flyer & things
10. Miss ___; vocal stylist who took care of Bud
12. ___ Janet; Momma
15. On the ___; running away
16. ___ Hoover; President of United States
19. HEC's instrument; a giant ___
20. Federal Bureau of Investigation
22. Gone = ___ (Rule 28)
23. Police stopped Lefty looking for ___ organizers
24. John ___; abolitionist

Bud, Not Buddy Crossword 1 Answer Key

							1 R		2 R				3 H		4 E
		5 S		6 C	L	A	R	E	N	C	E		8 R	E	A	D
9 S	H	E	D		A		P		D		O			R		D
U		E		10 T	R	A	I	N		11 P	E	12 A		M		I
I		D		H			D			S		N		A		E
T		13 S	T	O	N	E	S				14 G	U	N		
C				M		15 L		16 H	O	M	E				
A				17 A		G	R	A	C	E		18 L	E	19 F	T	Y
S		20 F	I	S	H			M		R		A		I		
E		B					21 B	U	22 D			I		D		
	23 L	I	24 B	R	A	R	Y		E			E		D		
	A		R						R			25 K	L	A	N	
	26 B	L	O	O	D				T			E			
	O		W												
27 G	R	A	N	D	F	A	T	H	E	R					

Across
6. Bud's pretend name at the mission
8. Momma ___ to Bud until he fell asleep
9. Where Amoses locked Bud
10. The boys wanted to hop on one going west
11. Sweet ___; restaurant
13. Had numbers & letters written on them
14. 1st part of the revenge plan was to get rid of this
16. Bud's word for the orphanage
17. Miss Thomas's first name
18. Mr. Lewis
20. Guards at the shed door
21. ____, Not Buddy
23. Bud looked for Miss Hill there
25. Ku Klux ____; organization against equal rights; members anonymous
26. Lefty was transporting this, so Bud thought he was a vampire
27. HEC to Bud

Down
1. Grand ____; where HEC lived
2. ___ caps; men who handled baggage at the train
3. Mr. Calloway's first name
4. Steady ____
5. Ideas are a lot like these
6. Bud tried to drive Lefty's away
7. They tried to keep the men off of the train
9. It held Bud's blanket, flyer & things
10. Miss ___; vocal stylist who took care of Bud
12. ____ Janet; Momma
15. On the ___; running away
16. ____ Hoover; President of United States
19. HEC's instrument; a giant ____
20. Federal Bureau of Investigation
22. Gone = ____ (Rule 28)
23. Police stopped Lefty looking for ___ organizers
24. John ____; abolitionist

Bud, Not Buddy Crossword 2

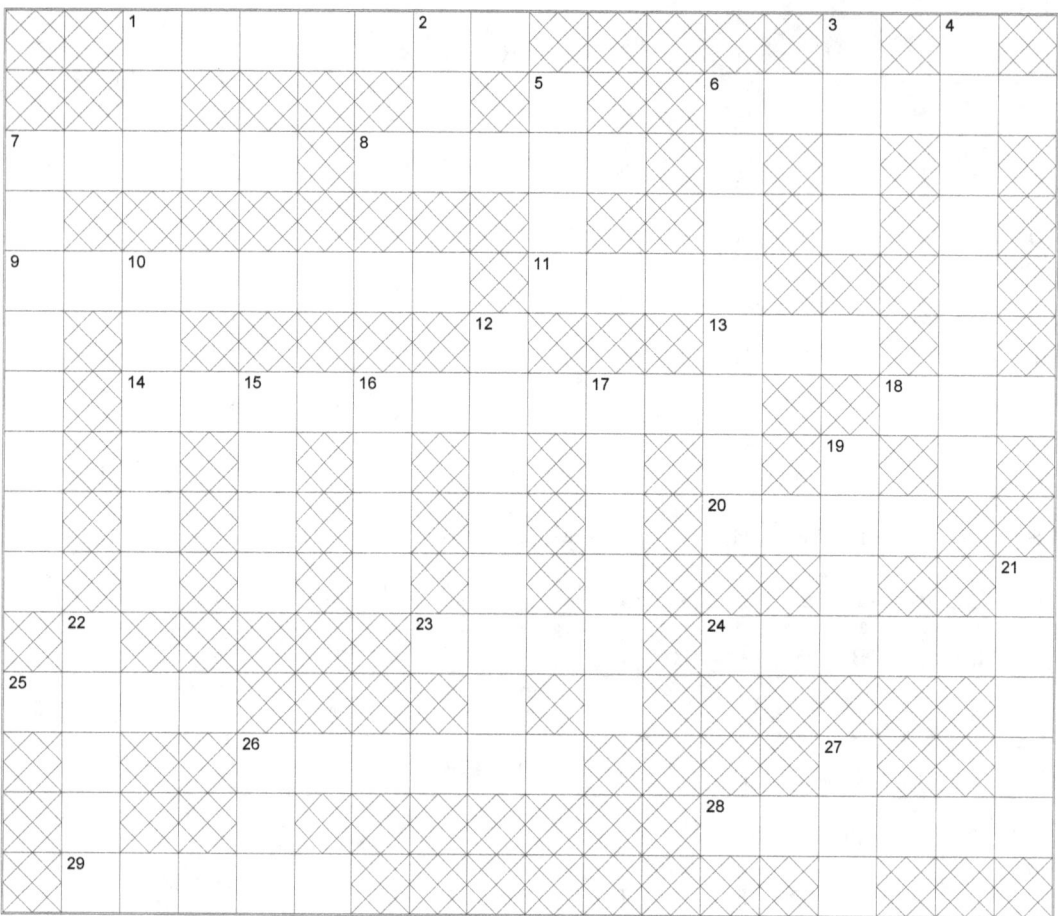

Across
1. Bud looked for Miss Hill there
6. Miss ___; vocal stylist who took care of Bud
7. She was unhappy at the Miss B. Gotten Moon Park
8. Steady ____
9. Bud's pretend name at the mission
11. Bud's word for the orphanage
13. 1st part of the revenge plan was to get rid of this
14. HEC to Bud
18. Bud tried to drive Lefty's away
20. Miss B. Gotten ____ Park
23. Miss Malone
24. Al ____; leader of Chicago underworld
25. Ku Klux ____; organization against equal rights; members anonymous
26. HEC's instrument; a giant ____
28. ___ LaBone; Bud
29. The boys wanted to hop on one going west

Down
1. On the ___; running away
2. ___ caps; men who handled baggage at the train
3. They tried to keep the men off of the train
4. Herman E. _____
5. Guards at the shed door
6. Lefty sent one to HEC, advising him of Bud's whereabouts
7. State where Bud lived
10. ____ Janet; Momma
12. Bud's last name
15. Mr. ___ locked Bud in the shed
16. Gone = ____ (Rule 28)
17. Mr. Calloway's first name
19. Whoop, _____, Sloop!
21. Machine Gun ____; gangster
22. Mrs. ___ was Lefty's daughter
26. Federal Bureau of Investigation
27. Sweet ___; restaurant

Bud, Not Buddy Crossword 2 Answer Key

			1 L	I	B	R	2 A	R	Y			3 C		4 C	
			A				E		5 F		6 T	H	O	M	A	S
7 M	O	M	M	A		8 E	D	D	I	E		E		P		L
I									S			L		S		L
9 C	L	10 A	R	E	N	C	E		11 H	O	M	E				O
H		N						12 C			13 G	U	N		W
I		14 G	R	15 A	N	16 D	F	A	17 T	H	E	R		18 C	A	R
G		E		M		E		L		E		A		19 Z		Y
A		L		O		A		D		R		20 M	O	O	N	
N		A		S		D		W		M				O		21 K
	22 S					23 D	E	Z	A		24 C	A	P	O	N	E
	25 K	L	A	N				L		N					L
	E			26 F	I	D	D	L	E			27 P		L
	E		B							28 S	L	E	E	P	Y
	29 T	R	A	I	N							A		

Across
1. Bud looked for Miss Hill there
6. Miss ___; vocal stylist who took care of Bud
7. She was unhappy at the Miss B. Gotten Moon Park
8. Steady ____
9. Bud's pretend name at the mission
11. Bud's word for the orphanage
13. 1st part of the revenge plan was to get rid of this
14. HEC to Bud
18. Bud tried to drive Lefty's away
20. Miss B. Gotten ____ Park
23. Miss Malone
24. Al ____; leader of Chicago underworld
25. Ku Klux ____; organization against equal rights; members anonymous
26. HEC's instrument; a giant ____
28. ___ LaBone; Bud
29. The boys wanted to hop on one going west

Down
1. On the ___; running away
2. ___ caps; men who handled baggage at the train
3. They tried to keep the men off of the train
4. Herman E. _____
5. Guards at the shed door
6. Lefty sent one to HEC, advising him of Bud's whereabouts
7. State where Bud lived
10. ____ Janet; Momma
12. Bud's last name
15. Mr. ___ locked Bud in the shed
16. Gone = ____ (Rule 28)
17. Mr. Calloway's first name
19. Whoop, _____, Sloop!
21. Machine Gun ____; gangster
22. Mrs. ___ was Lefty's daughter
26. Federal Bureau of Investigation
27. Sweet ___; restaurant

Bud, Not Buddy Crossword 3

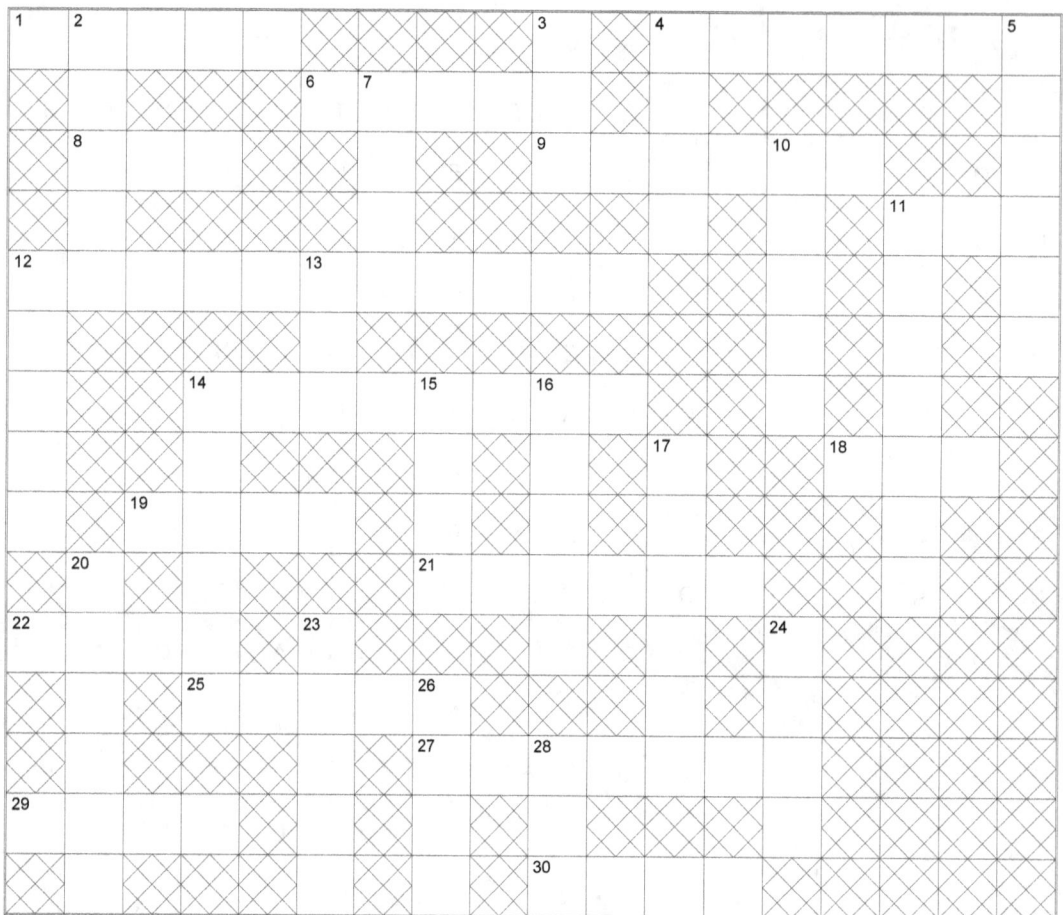

Across
1. Lefty was transporting this, so Bud thought he was a vampire
4. When wrapped in it, Bud felt close to Momma
6. Steady ____
8. ____, Not Buddy
9. ____ Janet; Momma
11. On the ___; running away
12. HEC to Bud
14. It held Bud's blanket, flyer & things
18. Bud tried to drive Lefty's away
19. Whoop, ____, Sloop!
21. ___ LaBone; Bud
22. Bud's word for the orphanage
25. Ideas are a lot like these
27. The vampire bat was actually this kind of a nest
29. Momma ___ to Bud until he fell asleep
30. Gone = ____ (Rule 28)

Down
2. Police stopped Lefty looking for ___ organizers
3. Sweet ___; restaurant
4. A cockroach crawled in his ear
5. Miss ___; vocal stylist who took care of Bud
7. Miss Malone
10. Mr. Lewis
11. Bud looked for Miss Hill there
12. Miss Thomas's first name
13. Federal Bureau of Investigation
14. Had numbers & letters written on them
15. They tried to keep the men off of the train
16. Mrs. ___ was Lefty's daughter
17. Al ____; leader of Chicago underworld
20. J. Edgar ____; head of FBI for 48 years
23. Machine Gun ____; gangster
24. Guards at the shed door
26. Where Amoses locked Bud
28. ___ caps; men who handled baggage at the train

Bud, Not Buddy Crossword 3 Answer Key

	1 B	2 L	O	O	D				3 P		4 B	L	A	N	K	E	5 T
		A					6 E	7 D	D	I	E						H
		8 B	U	D				E			9 A	N	G	E	10 L	A	O
		O						Z			S				E	11 L	A	M
	12 G	R	A	N	D	13 F	A	T	H	E	R				F	I		A
	R					B									T	B		S
	A		14 S	U	I	T	C	15 A	S	16 E					Y	R		
	C		T					O		L			17 C		18 C	A	R	
	E		19 Z	O	O	P		P		E			A			R		
		20 H		N			21 S	L	E	E	P	Y				Y		
	22 H	O	M	E		23 K				T			O		24 F			
		O		25 S	E	E	D	26 S					N		I			
		V				L		27 H	O	R	28 N	E	T	S				
	29 R	E	A	D		L		E			E				H			
		R				Y		30 D	E	A	D							

Across
1. Lefty was transporting this, so Bud thought he was a vampire
4. When wrapped in it, Bud felt close to Momma
6. Steady ____
8. ____, Not Buddy
9. ____ Janet; Momma
11. On the ___; running away
12. HEC to Bud
14. It held Bud's blanket, flyer & things
18. Bud tried to drive Lefty's away
19. Whoop, _____, Sloop!
21. ___ LaBone; Bud
22. Bud's word for the orphanage
25. Ideas are a lot like these
27. The vampire bat was actually this kind of a nest
29. Momma ___ to Bud until he fell asleep
30. Gone = ____ (Rule 28)

Down
2. Police stopped Lefty looking for ___ organizers
3. Sweet ___; restaurant
4. A cockroach crawled in his ear
5. Miss ___; vocal stylist who took care of Bud
7. Miss Malone
10. Mr. Lewis
11. Bud looked for Miss Hill there
12. Miss Thomas's first name
13. Federal Bureau of Investigation
14. Had numbers & letters written on them
15. They tried to keep the men off of the train
16. Mrs. ___ was Lefty's daughter
17. Al ____; leader of Chicago underworld
20. J. Edgar ____; head of FBI for 48 years
23. Machine Gun ____; gangster
24. Guards at the shed door
26. Where Amoses locked Bud
28. ___ caps; men who handled baggage at the train

Bud, Not Buddy Crossword 4

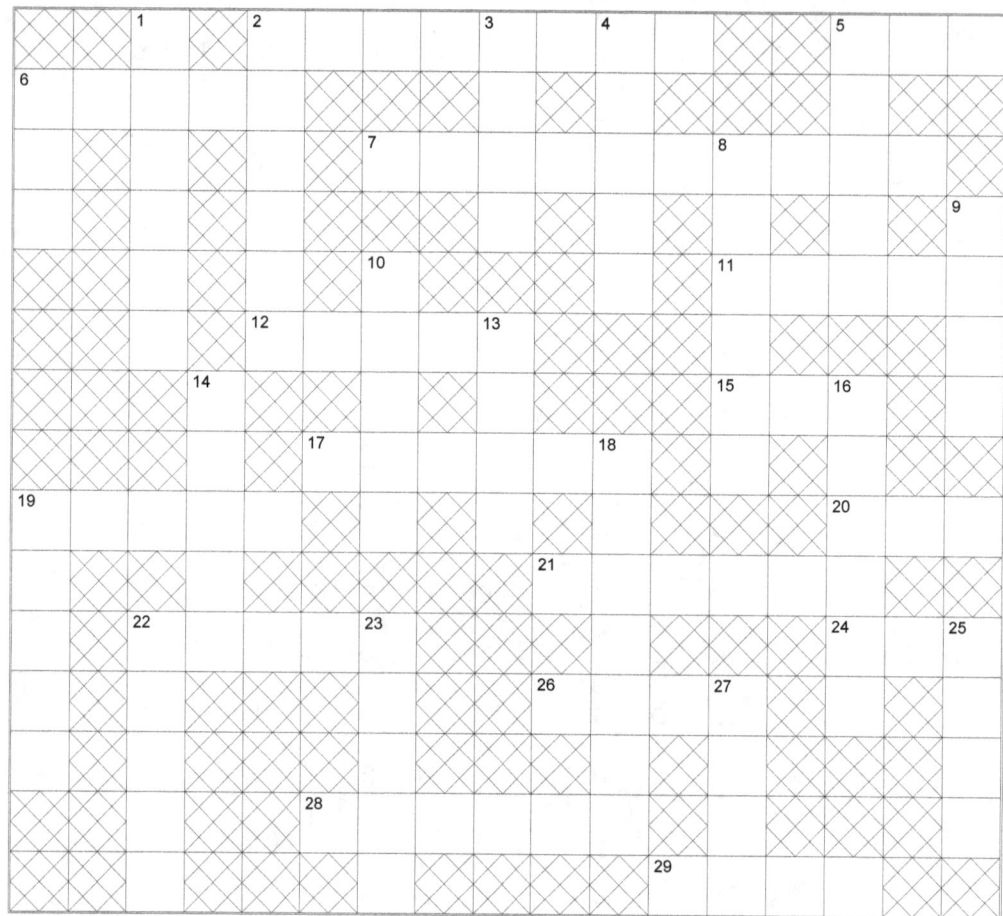

Across
2. It held Bud's blanket, flyer & things
5. ____, Not Buddy
6. City where Bud & Momma lived
7. HEC & The Dusky Devastators of the _____
11. Steady ____
12. Ideas are a lot like these
15. Sweet ___; restaurant
17. They had printed information about HEC and the band
19. Horn player who helped Bud
20. 1st part of the revenge plan was to get rid of this
21. Al ____; leader of Chicago underworld
22. Police stopped Lefty looking for ___ organizers
24. On the ___; running away
26. Guards at the shed door
28. Mr. Calloway's first name
29. Momma ___ to Bud until he fell asleep

Down
1. HEC's instrument; a giant ____
2. Had numbers & letters written on them
3. They tried to keep the men off of the train
4. Mrs. ___ was Lefty's daughter
5. Lefty was transporting this, so Bud thought he was a vampire
6. Federal Bureau of Investigation
8. ___ LaBone; Bud
9. Miss Malone
10. Machine Gun ____; gangster
13. Where Amoses locked Bud
14. She was unhappy at the Miss B. Gotten Moon Park
16. ____ Janet; Momma
18. Grand Calloway _____
19. He got a foster home with girls
22. Mr. Lewis
23. _____ & Things Number 328
25. Miss B. Gotten ____ Park
27. Bud's word for the orphanage

Bud, Not Buddy Crossword 4 Answer Key

	1 F	2 S	U	I	3 T	C	4 A	S	E		5 B	U	D
6 F	L	I	N	T			O		L		L		
B		D		O	7 D	E	P	R	E	S	S	I	O	N
I		D		O	N			S		E		L		O	9 D
		L			E		10 K			T		11 E	D	D	I	E
		E		12 S	E	E	D	S	13 S			E				Z
			14 M				L		H			15 P	E	16 A		A
			O		17 F	L	Y	E	R	S	18 S		Y		N	
19 J	I	M	M	Y		Y			D		T			20 G	U	N
E			M					21 C	A	P	O	N	E			
R	22 L	A	B	O	23 R						T			24 L	A	25 M
R	E				U			26 F	I	27 S	H			A		O
Y	F				L					O		O				O
	T			28 H	E	R	M	A	N			M				N
	Y				S					29 R	E	A	D			

Across
2. It held Bud's blanket, flyer & things
5. ____, Not Buddy
6. City where Bud & Momma lived
7. HEC & The Dusky Devastators of the _____
11. Steady ____
12. Ideas are a lot like these
15. Sweet ___; restaurant
17. They had printed information about HEC and the band
19. Horn player who helped Bud
20. 1st part of the revenge plan was to get rid of this
21. Al ____; leader of Chicago underworld
22. Police stopped Lefty looking for ___ organizers
24. On the ___; running away
26. Guards at the shed door
28. Mr. Calloway's first name
29. Momma ___ to Bud until he fell asleep

Down
1. HEC's instrument; a giant ____
2. Had numbers & letters written on them
3. They tried to keep the men off of the train
4. Mrs. ___ was Lefty's daughter
5. Lefty was transporting this, so Bud thought he was a vampire
6. Federal Bureau of Investigation
8. ___ LaBone; Bud
9. Miss Malone
10. Machine Gun ____; gangster
13. Where Amoses locked Bud
14. She was unhappy at the Miss B. Gotten Moon Park
16. ____ Janet; Momma
18. Grand Calloway _____
19. He got a foster home with girls
22. Mr. Lewis
23. _____ & Things Number 328
25. Miss B. Gotten ____ Park
27. Bud's word for the orphanage

Bud, Not Buddy

BUD	EDDIE	TELEGRAM	DEZA	ZOOP
DEAD	LABOR	RED	THOMAS	HERMAN
HORNETS	MOON	FREE SPACE	CLARENCE	BLANKET
GRACE	SLEEPY	HERBERT	RAPIDS	JIMMY
STATION	READ	BROWN	MISSION	GRANDFATHER

Bud, Not Buddy

SLEET	HOME	JERRY	RULES	CALDWELL
KELLY	FBI	FIDDLE	BLOOD	CALLOWAY
DEPRESSION	FLYERS	FREE SPACE	STONES	AMOS
DOOR	HOOVER	FLINT	SUITCASE	SAXOPHONE
SEEDS	MOMMA	CAPONE	TRAIN	KLAN

Bud, Not Buddy

JIMMY	SAXOPHONE	TRAIN	TEARS	FBI
HERMAN	THOMAS	COPS	CALDWELL	LABOR
CAPONE	MISSION	FREE SPACE	BUD	RED
HOOVERVILLE	DOOR	PEA	GRANDFATHER	READ
BLANKET	JERRY	CLARENCE	KLAN	HERBERT

Bud, Not Buddy

MICHIGAN	LAM	KELLY	RULES	MOMMA
BUGS	DEAD	FIDDLE	RAPIDS	HORNETS
DEPRESSION	AMOS	FREE SPACE	FLINT	GRACE
DEZA	STATION	ANGELA	SUITCASE	BROWN
STONES	BLOOD	EDDIE	SHED	SEEDS

Bud, Not Buddy

LAM	CAR	CLARENCE	BUD	LEFTY
HOOVER	MICHIGAN	SEEDS	FBI	STONES
MISSION	COPS	FREE SPACE	GUN	CAPONE
SLEET	BLOOD	STATION	EDDIE	SHED
RED	SLEEPY	ANGELA	HERMAN	RULES

Bud, Not Buddy

TEARS	MOON	KLAN	AMOS	DEZA
HOOVERVILLE	DEAD	LABOR	TRAIN	DEPRESSION
KELLY	TELEGRAM	FREE SPACE	READ	BLANKET
PEA	HORNETS	SAXOPHONE	FISH	RAPIDS
CALDWELL	FLINT	SUITCASE	BUGS	FLYERS

Bud, Not Buddy

PEA	LEFTY	GUN	EDDIE	CLARENCE
MISSION	DOOR	READ	SUITCASE	MICHIGAN
CAR	TEARS	FREE SPACE	JERRY	FLINT
KELLY	CALDWELL	GRACE	SHED	HERMAN
HOOVERVILLE	FBI	BUD	GRANDFATHER	ANGELA

Bud, Not Buddy

CALLOWAY	TELEGRAM	HORNETS	FLYERS	AMOS
DEAD	MOMMA	ZOOP	HOME	LABOR
THOMAS	HERBERT	FREE SPACE	BLANKET	COPS
RED	SEEDS	MOON	BUGS	KLAN
FIDDLE	SAXOPHONE	RULES	BROWN	DEPRESSION

Bud, Not Buddy

FIDDLE	CALDWELL	BUD	GRANDFATHER	TRAIN
HOOVER	KELLY	DEZA	MICHIGAN	ZOOP
GUN	LEFTY	FREE SPACE	FLINT	TEARS
AMOS	STONES	DOOR	SLEET	RAPIDS
EDDIE	SLEEPY	TELEGRAM	MISSION	SUITCASE

Bud, Not Buddy

CLARENCE	DEAD	HOME	STATION	SEEDS
MOON	CALLOWAY	BLOOD	FISH	ANGELA
FLYERS	SHED	FREE SPACE	HERMAN	COPS
CAPONE	READ	HOOVERVILLE	RULES	BLANKET
HERBERT	KLAN	DEPRESSION	FBI	PEA

Bud, Not Buddy

CALDWELL	TELEGRAM	BUGS	CAPONE	THOMAS
HERMAN	PEA	KLAN	LAM	COPS
DOOR	DEPRESSION	FREE SPACE	BUD	JERRY
HOOVER	READ	BLANKET	ZOOP	SUITCASE
EDDIE	MOON	FIDDLE	HERBERT	DEAD

Bud, Not Buddy

LABOR	FLYERS	RULES	RED	SAXOPHONE
LIBRARY	AMOS	CAR	GRANDFATHER	FISH
FLINT	SEEDS	FREE SPACE	MISSION	SLEEPY
STATION	RAPIDS	ANGELA	MICHIGAN	CLARENCE
DEZA	GRACE	SHED	SLEET	HORNETS

Bud, Not Buddy

SUITCASE	READ	LABOR	STATION	JIMMY
DOOR	GRACE	ZOOP	LEFTY	AMOS
MICHIGAN	MOON	FREE SPACE	RAPIDS	EDDIE
CALDWELL	JERRY	BROWN	BLOOD	CLARENCE
RULES	GUN	HOOVERVILLE	HORNETS	CAPONE

Bud, Not Buddy

TRAIN	DEPRESSION	SEEDS	SLEET	BLANKET
SHED	STONES	BUD	THOMAS	DEAD
GRANDFATHER	HERBERT	FREE SPACE	SAXOPHONE	FISH
KLAN	CALLOWAY	FLINT	PEA	LIBRARY
HOME	FLYERS	FBI	MOMMA	LAM

Bud, Not Buddy

TELEGRAM	HERMAN	SLEEPY	DOOR	MOON
SUITCASE	FLINT	GUN	FLYERS	CAPONE
STONES	RAPIDS	FREE SPACE	LEFTY	LABOR
DEAD	READ	CALLOWAY	FISH	DEPRESSION
BLOOD	RED	HORNETS	BLANKET	CLARENCE

Bud, Not Buddy

BROWN	JERRY	HOOVERVILLE	LAM	TEARS
KLAN	CAR	LIBRARY	DEZA	SAXOPHONE
TRAIN	EDDIE	FREE SPACE	ANGELA	PEA
AMOS	COPS	GRACE	SHED	SLEET
BUGS	GRANDFATHER	SEEDS	FIDDLE	RULES

Bud, Not Buddy

DEZA	SUITCASE	HERBERT	SEEDS	STONES
LIBRARY	CALDWELL	GRACE	RULES	JIMMY
SLEET	THOMAS	FREE SPACE	DEPRESSION	DEAD
STATION	CALLOWAY	TRAIN	HOOVERVILLE	BUGS
RED	READ	KELLY	HOME	SHED

Bud, Not Buddy

FBI	MISSION	SAXOPHONE	MOMMA	CAR
LABOR	DOOR	HOOVER	FISH	GUN
HERMAN	EDDIE	FREE SPACE	SLEEPY	BLOOD
COPS	HORNETS	KLAN	FIDDLE	CAPONE
FLINT	BLANKET	GRANDFATHER	PEA	LEFTY

Bud, Not Buddy

CAPONE	STONES	TELEGRAM	SLEEPY	TRAIN
CLARENCE	SAXOPHONE	EDDIE	BUGS	JERRY
HOOVERVILLE	RED	FREE SPACE	RAPIDS	HERMAN
CAR	MOON	BLOOD	FLINT	BROWN
LABOR	SEEDS	ANGELA	RULES	DOOR

Bud, Not Buddy

READ	HORNETS	JIMMY	FLYERS	FISH
SUITCASE	DEZA	KELLY	CALDWELL	HOOVER
BLANKET	THOMAS	FREE SPACE	CALLOWAY	FIDDLE
MISSION	AMOS	COPS	TEARS	DEPRESSION
HOME	LAM	MICHIGAN	SLEET	DEAD

Bud, Not Buddy

DEPRESSION	BLANKET	RULES	MICHIGAN	SHED
FLYERS	DEAD	HOOVER	PEA	STATION
LEFTY	GRACE	FREE SPACE	CALDWELL	MISSION
AMOS	LABOR	TEARS	LAM	COPS
SLEET	BROWN	BUGS	MOMMA	ZOOP

Bud, Not Buddy

LIBRARY	SEEDS	HERBERT	SLEEPY	CAR
THOMAS	GUN	READ	CLARENCE	KELLY
BUD	FLINT	FREE SPACE	CAPONE	DOOR
FISH	ANGELA	HOME	RAPIDS	KLAN
SAXOPHONE	CALLOWAY	EDDIE	TELEGRAM	JERRY

Bud, Not Buddy

CAPONE	HERMAN	FLINT	TELEGRAM	GRACE
ZOOP	HORNETS	LEFTY	FLYERS	LABOR
SLEET	LAM	FREE SPACE	MISSION	JIMMY
TEARS	DEAD	SLEEPY	DOOR	PEA
CLARENCE	RULES	TRAIN	HOOVERVILLE	FIDDLE

Bud, Not Buddy

BROWN	MICHIGAN	AMOS	RAPIDS	COPS
STATION	HOOVER	BLOOD	SHED	HOME
LIBRARY	KLAN	FREE SPACE	CAR	THOMAS
ANGELA	STONES	SUITCASE	JERRY	FBI
DEZA	BUGS	CALLOWAY	EDDIE	MOMMA

Bud, Not Buddy

FLYERS	AMOS	HERBERT	SEEDS	SUITCASE
MOMMA	SLEEPY	THOMAS	HOOVER	GRACE
JIMMY	CALDWELL	FREE SPACE	MOON	LIBRARY
READ	LAM	MICHIGAN	JERRY	RED
HORNETS	ZOOP	PEA	BLANKET	COPS

Bud, Not Buddy

CLARENCE	RAPIDS	BLOOD	LABOR	HERMAN
DEPRESSION	FIDDLE	LEFTY	GUN	MISSION
DOOR	EDDIE	FREE SPACE	KELLY	CAR
DEAD	FLINT	STATION	SAXOPHONE	SLEET
KLAN	TELEGRAM	BROWN	FBI	FISH

Bud, Not Buddy

MOMMA	DEZA	JERRY	RAPIDS	HERMAN
CALLOWAY	FISH	COPS	SHED	STONES
BLOOD	DEAD	FREE SPACE	BUD	BLANKET
STATION	MOON	AMOS	RULES	EDDIE
FLINT	SLEEPY	ANGELA	HOME	LABOR

Bud, Not Buddy

FBI	KLAN	TEARS	TELEGRAM	READ
SAXOPHONE	CLARENCE	CAR	HOOVERVILLE	DOOR
FLYERS	LIBRARY	FREE SPACE	FIDDLE	JIMMY
CAPONE	TRAIN	GRANDFATHER	GRACE	DEPRESSION
LAM	HORNETS	SUITCASE	MICHIGAN	CALDWELL

Bud, Not Buddy

FLYERS	AMOS	TEARS	BROWN	SLEEPY
COPS	HERMAN	BUGS	DEAD	HOOVERVILLE
JERRY	FBI	FREE SPACE	CALDWELL	DEPRESSION
KELLY	MICHIGAN	FISH	BUD	HERBERT
HOME	SLEET	THOMAS	FIDDLE	STATION

Bud, Not Buddy

EDDIE	KLAN	READ	BLANKET	CLARENCE
MOMMA	PEA	DOOR	JIMMY	MISSION
GRACE	LIBRARY	FREE SPACE	GRANDFATHER	CAR
HORNETS	SEEDS	BLOOD	TELEGRAM	TRAIN
ANGELA	FLINT	HOOVER	SUITCASE	LEFTY

Bud, Not Buddy

COPS	LABOR	AMOS	KLAN	BUD
SLEET	HOME	STATION	CAR	MISSION
CALDWELL	FISH	FREE SPACE	TELEGRAM	FLINT
BROWN	KELLY	SHED	READ	JERRY
MOMMA	BLANKET	PEA	GRANDFATHER	DOOR

Bud, Not Buddy

HOOVERVILLE	SEEDS	CLARENCE	CALLOWAY	HERMAN
RED	HERBERT	RULES	GRACE	TEARS
DEPRESSION	JIMMY	FREE SPACE	LEFTY	GUN
THOMAS	DEAD	FIDDLE	RAPIDS	MOON
HOOVER	SLEEPY	HORNETS	TRAIN	EDDIE

Bud, Not Buddy Vocabulary Word list

No.	Word	Clue/Definition
1.	ALIAS	A made-up name usually assumed to hide one's true identity
2.	APPRECIATE	Recognize something's value
3.	ASTHMA	Illness causing difficulty breathing
4.	CONCERN	Worry or care
5.	CONCLUSIONS	Results, decisions, deductions
6.	CONSIDERATE	Thinking of what will benefit others
7.	COPACETIC	Proper
8.	DECIDED	Chose
9.	DELICIOUS	Tastes good
10.	DEVOURED	Ate quickly and completely or hungrily
11.	ESPECIALLY	Particularly
12.	FIDGETING	Nervously moving about or twitching
13.	FOSTER	Temporary care
14.	FUMBLING	Clumsily searching
15.	GLUM	Sad
16.	HOODLUM	Small-time criminal
17.	HYPNOTIZING	Having the effect of putting one in a trance or asleep
18.	ILK	Kind, group, set
19.	INGRATITUDE	Attitude of being not thankful
20.	INSISTED	Repeatedly demanded
21.	KIN	Relative
22.	KNICKERS	Short pants
23.	LUGGED	Carried
24.	MATRIMONIAL	Relating to marriage
25.	MIDGET	Small in size
26.	MIRACLE	Act of God; something impossible happens
27.	MISSION	Charitable, usually religious, house for helping needy people
28.	NUDGED	Lightly or gently pushed
29.	OBVIOUS	Easy to see
30.	ORNERY	Not necessarily bad, but a trouble-maker
31.	PATIENT	Able to wait
32.	PRECIOUS	Valuable
33.	PROVOKED	Started; induced
34.	RADIATING	Shining, beaming, giving off rays
35.	RAID	Attack or invasion, sometimes to uncover something illegal
36.	RECOGNIZED	Identified
37.	REPUTATION	A person's character observed by others
38.	SACRIFICE	Hardship; giving up something
39.	SCOLDING	Lecturing; reprimanding
40.	SUSPICIOUS	Wary, not trusting
41.	TEMPERATURE	Hotness or coldness
42.	TEMPORARY	Not permanent; just for a while
43.	TOLERATE	Put up with; endure
44.	TORTURING	Mistreating; tormenting; abusing
45.	VEGETARIAN	Person who doesn't eat meat
46.	VENTRILOQUIST	Performer who can make the voice appear to come from somewhere else
47.	VERMIN	Low life creatures like rats

Bud, Not Buddy Vocabulary Fill In The Blanks 1

_____

_____

_____

_____

_____

_____

_____

_____

_____

_____

_____

_____

_____

_____

_____

_____

_____

_____

_____

_____

1. Repeatedly demanded
2. Charitable, usually religious, house for helping needy people
3. Shining, beaming, giving off rays
4. Chose
5. Particularly
6. Low life creatures like rats
7. A person's character observed by others
8. Identified
9. Results, decisions, deductions
10. Able to wait
11. Started; induced
12. Easy to see
13. Lightly or gently pushed
14. Small in size
15. Mistreating; tormenting; abusing
16. Recognize something's value
17. Clumsily searching
18. Lecturing; reprimanding
19. Hotness or coldness
20. Small-time criminal

Bud, Not Buddy Vocabulary Fill In The Blanks 1 Answer Key

INSISTED	1. Repeatedly demanded
MISSION	2. Charitable, usually religious, house for helping needy people
RADIATING	3. Shining, beaming, giving off rays
DECIDED	4. Chose
ESPECIALLY	5. Particularly
VERMIN	6. Low life creatures like rats
REPUTATION	7. A person's character observed by others
RECOGNIZED	8. Identified
CONCLUSIONS	9. Results, decisions, deductions
PATIENT	10. Able to wait
PROVOKED	11. Started; induced
OBVIOUS	12. Easy to see
NUDGED	13. Lightly or gently pushed
MIDGET	14. Small in size
TORTURING	15. Mistreating; tormenting; abusing
APPRECIATE	16. Recognize something's value
FUMBLING	17. Clumsily searching
SCOLDING	18. Lecturing; reprimanding
TEMPERATURE	19. Hotness or coldness
HOODLUM	20. Small-time criminal

Bud, Not Buddy Vocabulary Fill In The Blanks 2

_____

1. Sad

_____

2. Hotness or coldness

_____

3. Having the effect of putting one in a trance or asleep

_____

4. Hardship; giving up something

_____

5. Tastes good

_____

6. Attitude of being not thankful

_____

7. Put up with; endure

_____

8. Chose

_____

9. Charitable, usually religious, house for helping needy people

_____

10. Mistreating; tormenting; abusing

_____

11. Short pants

_____

12. Not permanent; just for a while

_____

13. Easy to see

_____

14. Performer who can make the voice appear to come from somewhere else

_____

15. Clumsily searching

_____

16. A made-up name usually assumed to hide one's true identity

_____

17. Low life creatures like rats

_____

18. Kind, group, set

_____

19. Relative

_____

20. Temporary care

Bud, Not Buddy Vocabulary Fill In The Blanks 2 Answer Key

GLUM	1. Sad
TEMPERATURE	2. Hotness or coldness
HYPNOTIZING	3. Having the effect of putting one in a trance or asleep
SACRIFICE	4. Hardship; giving up something
DELICIOUS	5. Tastes good
INGRATITUDE	6. Attitude of being not thankful
TOLERATE	7. Put up with; endure
DECIDED	8. Chose
MISSION	9. Charitable, usually religious, house for helping needy people
TORTURING	10. Mistreating; tormenting; abusing
KNICKERS	11. Short pants
TEMPORARY	12. Not permanent; just for a while
OBVIOUS	13. Easy to see
VENTRILOQUIST	14. Performer who can make the voice appear to come from somewhere else
FUMBLING	15. Clumsily searching
ALIAS	16. A made-up name usually assumed to hide one's true identity
VERMIN	17. Low life creatures like rats
ILK	18. Kind, group, set
KIN	19. Relative
FOSTER	20. Temporary care

Bud, Not Buddy Vocabulary Fill In The Blanks 3

_____

_____

_____

_____

_____

_____

_____

_____

_____

_____

_____

_____

_____

_____

_____

_____

_____

_____

_____

_____

1. Not necessarily bad, but a trouble-maker
2. Illness causing difficulty breathing
3. Clumsily searching
4. Having the effect of putting one in a trance or asleep
5. Able to wait
6. Repeatedly demanded
7. Mistreating; tormenting; abusing
8. Particularly
9. Shining, beaming, giving off rays
10. Person who doesn't eat meat
11. Charitable, usually religious, house for helping needy people
12. Attack or invasion, sometimes to uncover something illegal
13. A person's character observed by others
14. Temporary care
15. Sad
16. Hotness or coldness
17. Ate quickly and completely or hungrily
18. Carried
19. Act of God; something impossible happens
20. Worry or care

Bud, Not Buddy Vocabulary Fill In The Blanks 3 Answer Key

ORNERY	1. Not necessarily bad, but a trouble-maker
ASTHMA	2. Illness causing difficulty breathing
FUMBLING	3. Clumsily searching
HYPNOTIZING	4. Having the effect of putting one in a trance or asleep
PATIENT	5. Able to wait
INSISTED	6. Repeatedly demanded
TORTURING	7. Mistreating; tormenting; abusing
ESPECIALLY	8. Particularly
RADIATING	9. Shining, beaming, giving off rays
VEGETARIAN	10. Person who doesn't eat meat
MISSION	11. Charitable, usually religious, house for helping needy people
RAID	12. Attack or invasion, sometimes to uncover something illegal
REPUTATION	13. A person's character observed by others
FOSTER	14. Temporary care
GLUM	15. Sad
TEMPERATURE	16. Hotness or coldness
DEVOURED	17. Ate quickly and completely or hungrily
LUGGED	18. Carried
MIRACLE	19. Act of God; something impossible happens
CONCERN	20. Worry or care

Bud, Not Buddy Vocabulary Fill In The Blanks 4

_____ 1. Carried

_____ 2. Particularly

_____ 3. Results, decisions, deductions

_____ 4. Kind, group, set

_____ 5. Attitude of being not thankful

_____ 6. Clumsily searching

_____ 7. Lecturing; reprimanding

_____ 8. Relative

_____ 9. Short pants

_____ 10. Attack or invasion, sometimes to uncover something illegal

_____ 11. Chose

_____ 12. Illness causing difficulty breathing

_____ 13. Charitable, usually religious, house for helping needy people

_____ 14. Nervously moving about or twitching

_____ 15. Hotness or coldness

_____ 16. Started; induced

_____ 17. Hardship; giving up something

_____ 18. Identified

_____ 19. Valuable

_____ 20. Not permanent; just for a while

Bud, Not Buddy Vocabulary Fill In The Blanks 4 Answer Key

LUGGED	1. Carried
ESPECIALLY	2. Particularly
CONCLUSIONS	3. Results, decisions, deductions
ILK	4. Kind, group, set
INGRATITUDE	5. Attitude of being not thankful
FUMBLING	6. Clumsily searching
SCOLDING	7. Lecturing; reprimanding
KIN	8. Relative
KNICKERS	9. Short pants
RAID	10. Attack or invasion, sometimes to uncover something illegal
DECIDED	11. Chose
ASTHMA	12. Illness causing difficulty breathing
MISSION	13. Charitable, usually religious, house for helping needy people
FIDGETING	14. Nervously moving about or twitching
TEMPERATURE	15. Hotness or coldness
PROVOKED	16. Started; induced
SACRIFICE	17. Hardship; giving up something
RECOGNIZED	18. Identified
PRECIOUS	19. Valuable
TEMPORARY	20. Not permanent; just for a while

Bud, Not Buddy Vocabulary Matching 1

___ 1. OBVIOUS
___ 2. ILK
___ 3. GLUM
___ 4. FOSTER
___ 5. INSISTED
___ 6. RAID
___ 7. HOODLUM
___ 8. TEMPORARY
___ 9. RADIATING
___ 10. KIN
___ 11. DEVOURED
___ 12. SCOLDING
___ 13. MISSION
___ 14. LUGGED
___ 15. SACRIFICE
___ 16. TEMPERATURE
___ 17. DECIDED
___ 18. VERMIN
___ 19. NUDGED
___ 20. INGRATITUDE
___ 21. HYPNOTIZING
___ 22. RECOGNIZED
___ 23. VENTRILOQUIST
___ 24. DELICIOUS
___ 25. PATIENT

A. Repeatedly demanded
B. Small-time criminal
C. Having the effect of putting one in a trance or asleep
D. Charitable, usually religious, house for helping needy people
E. Lightly or gently pushed
F. Performer who can make the voice appear to come from somewhere else
G. Easy to see
H. Identified
I. Sad
J. Attitude of being not thankful
K. Kind, group, set
L. Ate quickly and completely or hungrily
M. Lecturing; reprimanding
N. Carried
O. Not permanent; just for a while
P. Relative
Q. Able to wait
R. Attack or invasion, sometimes to uncover something illegal
S. Hardship; giving up something
T. Hotness or coldness
U. Chose
V. Tastes good
W. Shining, beaming, giving off rays
X. Low life creatures like rats
Y. Temporary care

Bud, Not Buddy Vocabulary Matching 1 Answer Key

G - 1. OBVIOUS	A. Repeatedly demanded
K - 2. ILK	B. Small-time criminal
I - 3. GLUM	C. Having the effect of putting one in a trance or asleep
Y - 4. FOSTER	D. Charitable, usually religious, house for helping needy people
A - 5. INSISTED	E. Lightly or gently pushed
R - 6. RAID	F. Performer who can make the voice appear to come from somewhere else
B - 7. HOODLUM	G. Easy to see
O - 8. TEMPORARY	H. Identified
W - 9. RADIATING	I. Sad
P - 10. KIN	J. Attitude of being not thankful
L - 11. DEVOURED	K. Kind, group, set
M - 12. SCOLDING	L. Ate quickly and completely or hungrily
D - 13. MISSION	M. Lecturing; reprimanding
N - 14. LUGGED	N. Carried
S - 15. SACRIFICE	O. Not permanent; just for a while
T - 16. TEMPERATURE	P. Relative
U - 17. DECIDED	Q. Able to wait
X - 18. VERMIN	R. Attack or invasion, sometimes to uncover something illegal
E - 19. NUDGED	S. Hardship; giving up something
J - 20. INGRATITUDE	T. Hotness or coldness
C - 21. HYPNOTIZING	U. Chose
H - 22. RECOGNIZED	V. Tastes good
F - 23. VENTRILOQUIST	W. Shining, beaming, giving off rays
V - 24. DELICIOUS	X. Low life creatures like rats
Q - 25. PATIENT	Y. Temporary care

Bud, Not Buddy Vocabulary Matching 2

___ 1. SUSPICIOUS A. Clumsily searching
___ 2. TOLERATE B. Tastes good
___ 3. VERMIN C. Particularly
___ 4. INSISTED D. Thinking of what will benefit others
___ 5. GLUM E. Put up with; endure
___ 6. COPACETIC F. Low life creatures like rats
___ 7. PRECIOUS G. Valuable
___ 8. INGRATITUDE H. Performer who can make the voice appear to come from somewhere else
___ 9. DELICIOUS I. Proper
___10. DECIDED J. Chose
___11. FUMBLING K. A made-up name usually assumed to hide one's true identity
___12. VENTRILOQUIST L. Person who doesn't eat meat
___13. MIRACLE M. Mistreating; tormenting; abusing
___14. OBVIOUS N. Started; induced
___15. MIDGET O. Repeatedly demanded
___16. SACRIFICE P. Kind, group, set
___17. ALIAS Q. Hardship; giving up something
___18. ESPECIALLY R. Lecturing; reprimanding
___19. CONSIDERATE S. Attitude of being not thankful
___20. ILK T. Act of God; something impossible happens
___21. VEGETARIAN U. Sad
___22. TORTURING V. Easy to see
___23. CONCLUSIONS W. Results, decisions, deductions
___24. SCOLDING X. Wary, not trusting
___25. PROVOKED Y. Small in size

Bud, Not Buddy Vocabulary Matching 2 Answer Key

X - 1. SUSPICIOUS
E - 2. TOLERATE
F - 3. VERMIN
O - 4. INSISTED
U - 5. GLUM
I - 6. COPACETIC
G - 7. PRECIOUS
S - 8. INGRATITUDE
B - 9. DELICIOUS
J - 10. DECIDED
A - 11. FUMBLING
H - 12. VENTRILOQUIST
T - 13. MIRACLE
V - 14. OBVIOUS
Y - 15. MIDGET
Q - 16. SACRIFICE
K - 17. ALIAS
C - 18. ESPECIALLY
D - 19. CONSIDERATE
P - 20. ILK
L - 21. VEGETARIAN
M - 22. TORTURING
W - 23. CONCLUSIONS
R - 24. SCOLDING
N - 25. PROVOKED

A. Clumsily searching
B. Tastes good
C. Particularly
D. Thinking of what will benefit others
E. Put up with; endure
F. Low life creatures like rats
G. Valuable
H. Performer who can make the voice appear to come from somewhere else
I. Proper
J. Chose
K. A made-up name usually assumed to hide one's true identity
L. Person who doesn't eat meat
M. Mistreating; tormenting; abusing
N. Started; induced
O. Repeatedly demanded
P. Kind, group, set
Q. Hardship; giving up something
R. Lecturing; reprimanding
S. Attitude of being not thankful
T. Act of God; something impossible happens
U. Sad
V. Easy to see
W. Results, decisions, deductions
X. Wary, not trusting
Y. Small in size

Bud, Not Buddy Vocabulary Matching 3

___ 1. DECIDED A. Chose
___ 2. FOSTER B. Small-time criminal
___ 3. ALIAS C. Temporary care
___ 4. COPACETIC D. Worry or care
___ 5. INGRATITUDE E. Wary, not trusting
___ 6. APPRECIATE F. Attitude of being not thankful
___ 7. HOODLUM G. Tastes good
___ 8. NUDGED H. Illness causing difficulty breathing
___ 9. GLUM I. Nervously moving about or twitching
___ 10. TEMPERATURE J. Sad
___ 11. ASTHMA K. Lightly or gently pushed
___ 12. RADIATING L. Repeatedly demanded
___ 13. MATRIMONIAL M. Relating to marriage
___ 14. PROVOKED N. Relative
___ 15. FIDGETING O. Started; induced
___ 16. KIN P. Small in size
___ 17. MIDGET Q. Hotness or coldness
___ 18. DELICIOUS R. Not permanent; just for a while
___ 19. TEMPORARY S. A person's character observed by others
___ 20. SACRIFICE T. A made-up name usually assumed to hide one's true identity
___ 21. INSISTED U. Shining, beaming, giving off rays
___ 22. REPUTATION V. Recognize something's value
___ 23. RECOGNIZED W. Identified
___ 24. CONCERN X. Hardship; giving up something
___ 25. SUSPICIOUS Y. Proper

Bud, Not Buddy Vocabulary Matching 3 Answer Key

A - 1. DECIDED		A. Chose
C - 2. FOSTER		B. Small-time criminal
T - 3. ALIAS		C. Temporary care
Y - 4. COPACETIC		D. Worry or care
F - 5. INGRATITUDE		E. Wary, not trusting
V - 6. APPRECIATE		F. Attitude of being not thankful
B - 7. HOODLUM		G. Tastes good
K - 8. NUDGED		H. Illness causing difficulty breathing
J - 9. GLUM		I. Nervously moving about or twitching
Q -10. TEMPERATURE		J. Sad
H -11. ASTHMA		K. Lightly or gently pushed
U -12. RADIATING		L. Repeatedly demanded
M -13. MATRIMONIAL		M. Relating to marriage
O -14. PROVOKED		N. Relative
I - 15. FIDGETING		O. Started; induced
N -16. KIN		P. Small in size
P -17. MIDGET		Q. Hotness or coldness
G -18. DELICIOUS		R. Not permanent; just for a while
R -19. TEMPORARY		S. A person's character observed by others
X -20. SACRIFICE		T. A made-up name usually assumed to hide one's true identity
L -21. INSISTED		U. Shining, beaming, giving off rays
S -22. REPUTATION		V. Recognize something's value
W -23. RECOGNIZED		W. Identified
D -24. CONCERN		X. Hardship; giving up something
E -25. SUSPICIOUS		Y. Proper

Bud, Not Buddy Vocabulary Matching 4

___ 1. VENTRILOQUIST   A. Chose
___ 2. PROVOKED   B. Able to wait
___ 3. DECIDED   C. Tastes good
___ 4. MIDGET   D. Not necessarily bad, but a trouble-maker
___ 5. TEMPERATURE   E. Nervously moving about or twitching
___ 6. APPRECIATE   F. Started; induced
___ 7. VERMIN   G. Identified
___ 8. HOODLUM   H. Kind, group, set
___ 9. OBVIOUS   I. Having the effect of putting one in a trance or asleep
___ 10. DELICIOUS   J. A made-up name usually assumed to hide one's true identity
___ 11. SACRIFICE   K. Thinking of what will benefit others
___ 12. PATIENT   L. Recognize something's value
___ 13. CONSIDERATE   M. A person's character observed by others
___ 14. HYPNOTIZING   N. Wary, not trusting
___ 15. RECOGNIZED   O. Performer who can make the voice appear to come from somewhere else
___ 16. SUSPICIOUS   P. Hotness or coldness
___ 17. ILK   Q. Easy to see
___ 18. KNICKERS   R. Low life creatures like rats
___ 19. TORTURING   S. Hardship; giving up something
___ 20. ALIAS   T. Small in size
___ 21. REPUTATION   U. Worry or care
___ 22. ORNERY   V. Mistreating; tormenting; abusing
___ 23. CONCERN   W. Small-time criminal
___ 24. VEGETARIAN   X. Short pants
___ 25. FIDGETING   Y. Person who doesn't eat meat

Bud, Not Buddy Vocabulary Matching 4 Answer Key

O - 1. VENTRILOQUIST　　A. Chose
F - 2. PROVOKED　　B. Able to wait
A - 3. DECIDED　　C. Tastes good
T - 4. MIDGET　　D. Not necessarily bad, but a trouble-maker
P - 5. TEMPERATURE　　E. Nervously moving about or twitching
L - 6. APPRECIATE　　F. Started; induced
R - 7. VERMIN　　G. Identified
W - 8. HOODLUM　　H. Kind, group, set
Q - 9. OBVIOUS　　I. Having the effect of putting one in a trance or asleep
C - 10. DELICIOUS　　J. A made-up name usually assumed to hide one's true identity
S - 11. SACRIFICE　　K. Thinking of what will benefit others
B - 12. PATIENT　　L. Recognize something's value
K - 13. CONSIDERATE　　M. A person's character observed by others
I - 14. HYPNOTIZING　　N. Wary, not trusting
G - 15. RECOGNIZED　　O. Performer who can make the voice appear to come from somewhere else
N - 16. SUSPICIOUS　　P. Hotness or coldness
H - 17. ILK　　Q. Easy to see
X - 18. KNICKERS　　R. Low life creatures like rats
V - 19. TORTURING　　S. Hardship; giving up something
J - 20. ALIAS　　T. Small in size
M - 21. REPUTATION　　U. Worry or care
D - 22. ORNERY　　V. Mistreating; tormenting; abusing
U - 23. CONCERN　　W. Small-time criminal
Y - 24. VEGETARIAN　　X. Short pants
E - 25. FIDGETING　　Y. Person who doesn't eat meat

Bud, Not Buddy Vocabulary Magic Squares 1

Match the definition with the vocabulary word. Put your answers in the magic squares below. When your answers are correct, all columns and rows will add to the same number.

A. FIDGETING
B. DEVOURED
C. DELICIOUS
D. CONCLUSIONS
E. FOSTER
F. PROVOKED
G. FUMBLING
H. RAID
I. GLUM
J. TOLERATE
K. HYPNOTIZING
L. KIN
M. MATRIMONIAL
N. HOODLUM
O. INSISTED
P. VENTRILOQUIST

1. Repeatedly demanded
2. Put up with; endure
3. Attack or invasion, sometimes to uncover something illegal
4. Nervously moving about or twitching
5. Results, decisions, deductions
6. Temporary care
7. Having the effect of putting one in a trance or asleep
8. Small-time criminal
9. Started; induced
10. Tastes good
11. Relating to marriage
12. Relative
13. Sad
14. Performer who can make the voice appear to come from somewhere else
15. Ate quickly and completely or hungrily
16. Clumsily searching

A=	B=	C=	D=
E=	F=	G=	H=
I=	J=	K=	L=
M=	N=	O=	P=

Bud, Not Buddy Vocabulary Magic Squares 1 Answer Key

Match the definition with the vocabulary word. Put your answers in the magic squares below. When your answers are correct, all columns and rows will add to the same number.

A. FIDGETING
B. DEVOURED
C. DELICIOUS
D. CONCLUSIONS
E. FOSTER
F. PROVOKED
G. FUMBLING
H. RAID
I. GLUM
J. TOLERATE
K. HYPNOTIZING
L. KIN
M. MATRIMONIAL
N. HOODLUM
O. INSISTED
P. VENTRILOQUIST

1. Repeatedly demanded
2. Put up with; endure
3. Attack or invasion, sometimes to uncover something illegal
4. Nervously moving about or twitching
5. Results, decisions, deductions
6. Temporary care
7. Having the effect of putting one in a trance or asleep
8. Small-time criminal
9. Started; induced
10. Tastes good
11. Relating to marriage
12. Relative
13. Sad
14. Performer who can make the voice appear to come from somewhere else
15. Ate quickly and completely or hungrily
16. Clumsily searching

A=4	B=15	C=10	D=5
E=6	F=9	G=16	H=3
I=13	J=2	K=7	L=12
M=11	N=8	O=1	P=14

Bud, Not Buddy Vocabulary Magic Squares 2

Match the definition with the vocabulary word. Put your answers in the magic squares below. When your answers are correct, all columns and rows will add to the same number.

A. TEMPORARY
B. COPACETIC
C. TOLERATE
D. CONSIDERATE
E. INGRATITUDE
F. PRECIOUS
G. TORTURING
H. ASTHMA
I. MATRIMONIAL
J. VERMIN
K. ESPECIALLY
L. DELICIOUS
M. FUMBLING
N. MISSION
O. RADIATING
P. GLUM

1. Illness causing difficulty breathing
2. Clumsily searching
3. Proper
4. Particularly
5. Low life creatures like rats
6. Put up with; endure
7. Sad
8. Attitude of being not thankful
9. Shining, beaming, giving off rays
10. Valuable
11. Relating to marriage
12. Thinking of what will benefit others
13. Not permanent; just for a while
14. Tastes good
15. Mistreating; tormenting; abusing
16. Charitable, usually religious, house for helping needy people

A=	B=	C=	D=
E=	F=	G=	H=
I=	J=	K=	L=
M=	N=	O=	P=

Bud, Not Buddy Vocabulary Magic Squares 2 Answer Key

Match the definition with the vocabulary word. Put your answers in the magic squares below. When your answers are correct, all columns and rows will add to the same number.

A. TEMPORARY
B. COPACETIC
C. TOLERATE
D. CONSIDERATE
E. INGRATITUDE
F. PRECIOUS
G. TORTURING
H. ASTHMA
I. MATRIMONIAL
J. VERMIN
K. ESPECIALLY
L. DELICIOUS
M. FUMBLING
N. MISSION
O. RADIATING
P. GLUM

1. Illness causing difficulty breathing
2. Clumsily searching
3. Proper
4. Particularly
5. Low life creatures like rats
6. Put up with; endure
7. Sad
8. Attitude of being not thankful
9. Shining, beaming, giving off rays
10. Valuable
11. Relating to marriage
12. Thinking of what will benefit others
13. Not permanent; just for a while
14. Tastes good
15. Mistreating; tormenting; abusing
16. Charitable, usually religious, house for helping needy people

A=13	B=3	C=6	D=12
E=8	F=10	G=15	H=1
I=11	J=5	K=4	L=14
M=2	N=16	O=9	P=7

Bud, Not Buddy Vocabulary Magic Squares 3

Match the definition with the vocabulary word. Put your answers in the magic squares below. When your answers are correct, all columns and rows will add to the same number.

A. TEMPERATURE
B. HOODLUM
C. FIDGETING
D. INGRATITUDE
E. KIN
F. ALIAS
G. PATIENT
H. COPACETIC
I. OBVIOUS
J. MIDGET
K. FOSTER
L. INSISTED
M. LUGGED
N. FUMBLING
O. RECOGNIZED
P. ORNERY

1. Carried
2. A made-up name usually assumed to hide one's true identity
3. Proper
4. Identified
5. Repeatedly demanded
6. Nervously moving about or twitching
7. Hotness or coldness
8. Small in size
9. Temporary care
10. Attitude of being not thankful
11. Small-time criminal
12. Easy to see
13. Clumsily searching
14. Relative
15. Able to wait
16. Not necessarily bad, but a trouble-maker

A= 7	B= 11	C= 6	D= 10
E= 14	F= 2	G= 15	H= 3
I= 12	J= 8	K= 9	L= 5
M= 1	N= 13	O= 4	P= 16

Bud, Not Buddy Vocabulary Magic Squares 3 Answer Key

Match the definition with the vocabulary word. Put your answers in the magic squares below. When your answers are correct, all columns and rows will add to the same number.

A. TEMPERATURE
B. HOODLUM
C. FIDGETING
D. INGRATITUDE
E. KIN
F. ALIAS
G. PATIENT
H. COPACETIC
I. OBVIOUS
J. MIDGET
K. FOSTER
L. INSISTED
M. LUGGED
N. FUMBLING
O. RECOGNIZED
P. ORNERY

1. Carried
2. A made-up name usually assumed to hide one's true identity
3. Proper
4. Identified
5. Repeatedly demanded
6. Nervously moving about or twitching
7. Hotness or coldness
8. Small in size
9. Temporary care
10. Attitude of being not thankful
11. Small-time criminal
12. Easy to see
13. Clumsily searching
14. Relative
15. Able to wait
16. Not necessarily bad, but a trouble-maker

A=7	B=11	C=6	D=10
E=14	F=2	G=15	H=3
I=12	J=8	K=9	L=5
M=1	N=13	O=4	P=16

Bud, Not Buddy Vocabulary Magic Squares 4

Match the definition with the vocabulary word. Put your answers in the magic squares below. When your answers are correct, all columns and rows will add to the same number.

A. FUMBLING
B. MIRACLE
C. RAID
D. ESPECIALLY
E. TOLERATE
F. SCOLDING
G. KNICKERS
H. FIDGETING
I. HYPNOTIZING
J. CONCLUSIONS
K. PATIENT
L. COPACETIC
M. ILK
N. GLUM
O. INSISTED
P. ASTHMA

1. Nervously moving about or twitching
2. Clumsily searching
3. Act of God; something impossible happens
4. Short pants
5. Results, decisions, deductions
6. Repeatedly demanded
7. Illness causing difficulty breathing
8. Having the effect of putting one in a trance or asleep
9. Able to wait
10. Sad
11. Kind, group, set
12. Proper
13. Put up with; endure
14. Particularly
15. Attack or invasion, sometimes to uncover something illegal
16. Lecturing; reprimanding

A=	B=	C=	D=
E=	F=	G=	H=
I=	J=	K=	L=
M=	N=	O=	P=

Bud, Not Buddy Vocabulary Magic Squares 4 Answer Key

Match the definition with the vocabulary word. Put your answers in the magic squares below. When your answers are correct, all columns and rows will add to the same number.

A. FUMBLING
B. MIRACLE
C. RAID
D. ESPECIALLY
E. TOLERATE
F. SCOLDING
G. KNICKERS
H. FIDGETING
I. HYPNOTIZING
J. CONCLUSIONS
K. PATIENT
L. COPACETIC
M. ILK
N. GLUM
O. INSISTED
P. ASTHMA

1. Nervously moving about or twitching
2. Clumsily searching
3. Act of God; something impossible happens
4. Short pants
5. Results, decisions, deductions
6. Repeatedly demanded
7. Illness causing difficulty breathing
8. Having the effect of putting one in a trance or asleep
9. Able to wait
10. Sad
11. Kind, group, set
12. Proper
13. Put up with; endure
14. Particularly
15. Attack or invasion, sometimes to uncover something illegal
16. Lecturing; reprimanding

A=2	B=3	C=15	D=14
E=13	F=16	G=4	H=1
I=8	J=5	K=9	L=12
M=11	N=10	O=6	P=7

Bud, Not Buddy Vocabulary Word Search 1

```
V I N G R A T I T U D E Z I N G O C E R W
Y E C Z P N N Y L L A I C E P S E H R G M
Z G G P L Q R K M J M R M R T F Z H E B L
Y J F E R A D I A T I N G U O M Q T P A Z
V K X D T O N G D C R W Z T R R K T U P Y
P M S T Q A V R C P A Q P A T R P E T P N
K S N M D M R O L Q C A J R U D L M A R J
V X Z J E Q N I K R L S F E R E Z P T E H
M E B W L Y J D A E E T S P I G G O I C K
Z C R W I O E L D N D H P M N G V R O I R
M L V M C D R G M K Q M R E G U K A N A G
M A T R I M O N I A L A X T O L E R A T E
H Q K C O N N I E H G S I K I T E Y X E M
Y P E J U D D D D R C H X N A T M N C K L
P D A M S X L L P R Y O L R S D O O J I G
N R G T W S U O I V B O E O D I P Y R N N
O U W L I C J C D C B D F E S A S S I T V
T Y D X U E Z S C G I L R S C R R T Z E M
I A Z G F M N Z O S J U I E S E E X E G X
Z S L Z E D L T N M O M T G K G Q F Y D G
I V Y I B D P O C V Y I T C D V H J W I B
N N S D A D C R E D C L I I Z Q K J X M S
G C Q L C S S D R J C N F U M B L I N G B
P R E C I O U S N C K S A C R I F I C E R
```

A made-up name usually assumed to hide one's true identity (5)
A person's character observed by others (10)
Able to wait (7)
Act of God; something impossible happens (7)
Ate quickly and completely or hungrily (8)
Attack or invasion, sometimes to uncover something illegal (4)
Attitude of being not thankful (11)
Carried (6)
Charitable, usually religious, house for helping needy people (7)
Chose (7)
Clumsily searching (8)
Easy to see (7)
Hardship; giving up something (9)
Having the effect of putting one in a trance or asleep (11)
Hotness or coldness (11)
Identified (10)
Illness causing difficulty breathing (6)
Kind, group, set (3)
Lecturing; reprimanding (8)
Lightly or gently pushed (6)
Low life creatures like rats (6)
Mistreating; tormenting; abusing (9)
Nervously moving about or twitching (9)
Not necessarily bad, but a trouble-maker (6)
Not permanent; just for a while (9)
Particularly (10)
Person who doesn't eat meat (10)
Proper (9)
Put up with; endure (8)
Recognize something's value (10)
Relating to marriage (11)
Relative (3)
Repeatedly demanded (8)
Sad (4)
Shining, beaming, giving off rays (9)
Short pants (8)
Small in size (6)
Small-time criminal (7)
Started; induced (8)
Tastes good (9)
Temporary care (6)
Thinking of what will benefit others (11)
Valuable (8)
Worry or care (7)

Bud, Not Buddy Vocabulary Word Search 1 Answer Key

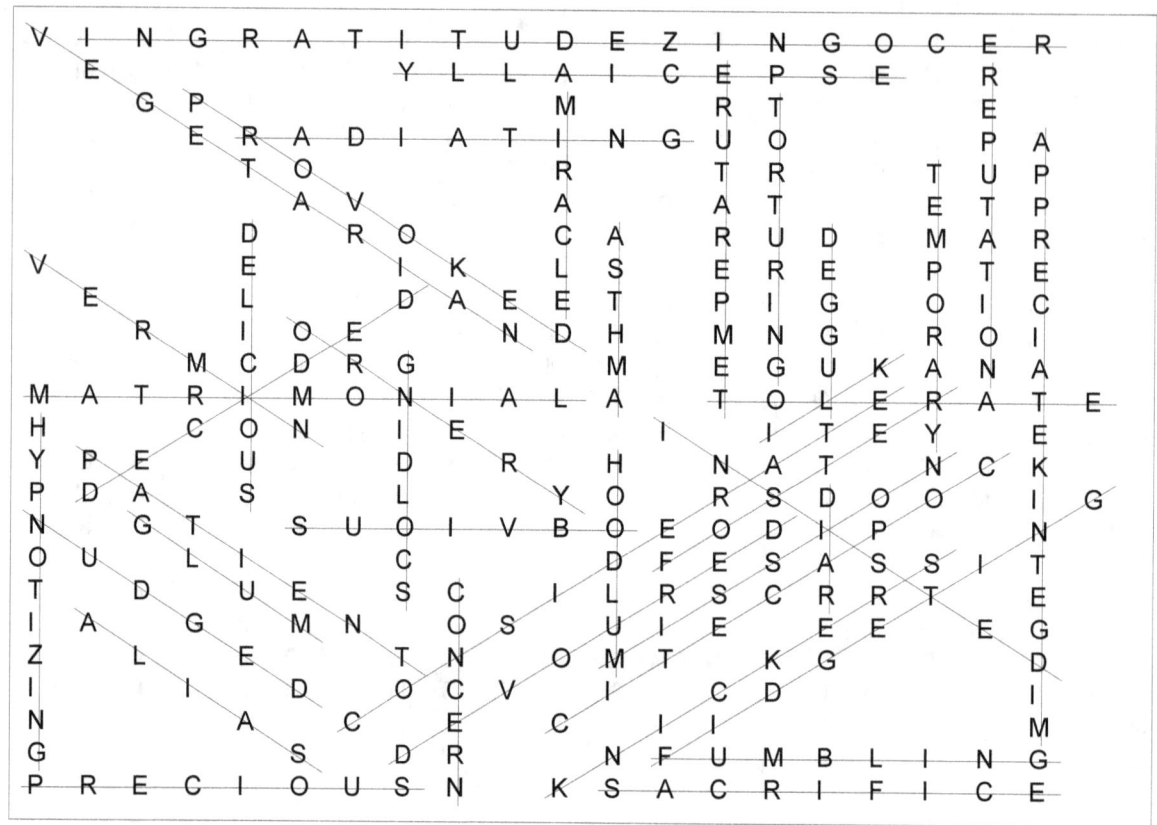

A made-up name usually assumed to hide one's true identity (5)
A person's character observed by others (10)
Able to wait (7)
Act of God; something impossible happens (7)
Ate quickly and completely or hungrily (8)
Attack or invasion, sometimes to uncover something illegal (4)
Attitude of being not thankful (11)
Carried (6)
Charitable, usually religious, house for helping needy people (7)
Chose (7)
Clumsily searching (8)
Easy to see (7)
Hardship; giving up something (9)
Having the effect of putting one in a trance or asleep (11)
Hotness or coldness (11)
Identified (10)
Illness causing difficulty breathing (6)
Kind, group, set (3)
Lecturing; reprimanding (8)
Lightly or gently pushed (6)
Low life creatures like rats (6)
Mistreating; tormenting; abusing (9)
Nervously moving about or twitching (9)
Not necessarily bad, but a trouble-maker (6)
Not permanent; just for a while (9)
Particularly (10)
Person who doesn't eat meat (10)
Proper (9)
Put up with; endure (8)
Recognize something's value (10)
Relating to marriage (11)
Relative (3)
Repeatedly demanded (8)
Sad (4)
Shining, beaming, giving off rays (9)
Short pants (8)
Small in size (6)
Small-time criminal (7)
Started; induced (8)
Tastes good (9)
Temporary care (6)
Thinking of what will benefit others (11)
Valuable (8)
Worry or care (7)

Bud, Not Buddy Vocabulary Word Search 2

```
D V C O F U M B L I N G M R F B I C H T H
E C D B S S U O I C I L E D N B N O C O T
C O Q V N Y S U S P I C I O U S S N X R D
I P H I K P S X C H O E Y N M X I C E T X
D A K O W B A V C G Y S Z F H N S L T U X
E C Q U V N D S N D R P B N P O T U A R F
D E B S R H Q I T Z S E N L P I E S R I T
H T F S A B Z P M H J C V O G S D I E N M
P I X I I E T Z S W M I K D T S N O L G L
S C O L D I N G V E T A R E D I S N O C X
A N K D Q G D T X T P L D H K M Z S T G O
C L N M E S E Q S P Z L F O P W I I F R C
R P I L X V D T R C W Y V O M U L G N B S
I A C A R P O E I O F V E D S I K E P G L
F T K Q S F C U C N R E L T T R B R L M
I I E L K I D K R C G M U E Y E A E Y V
C E R H A H L P D E G E I M M P Y R C W X
  E N S T V J C E D R D T N V P R D P I L B
B T E T J D G P T N R A N M O O J D O F E
R Q K F E D T E Z G S R X G R V L H U D S
T C J G U M G Z R J S I B T A O Y N S X V
H F G N C D H B V W G A B M R K Y N M X H
R U G N I T A I D A R N D S Y E F B P Z Z
L P Q M R E P U T A T I O N W D R H B B P
```

A made-up name usually assumed to hide one's true identity (5)
A person's character observed by others (10)
Able to wait (7)
Act of God; something impossible happens (7)
Ate quickly and completely or hungrily (8)
Attack or invasion, sometimes to uncover something illegal (4)
Carried (6)
Charitable, usually religious, house for helping needy people (7)
Chose (7)
Clumsily searching (8)
Easy to see (7)
Hardship; giving up something (9)
Having the effect of putting one in a trance or asleep (11)
Identified (10)
Illness causing difficulty breathing (6)
Kind, group, set (3)
Lecturing; reprimanding (8)
Lightly or gently pushed (6)
Low life creatures like rats (6)
Mistreating; tormenting; abusing (9)
Nervously moving about or twitching (9)
Not necessarily bad, but a trouble-maker (6)
Not permanent; just for a while (9)
Particularly (10)
Person who doesn't eat meat (10)
Proper (9)
Put up with; endure (8)
Recognize something's value (10)
Relative (3)
Repeatedly demanded (8)
Results, decisions, deductions (11)
Sad (4)
Shining, beaming, giving off rays (9)
Short pants (8)
Small in size (6)
Small-time criminal (7)
Started; induced (8)
Tastes good (9)
Temporary care (6)
Thinking of what will benefit others (11)
Valuable (8)
Wary, not trusting (10)
Worry or care (7)

Bud, Not Buddy Vocabulary Word Search 2 Answer Key

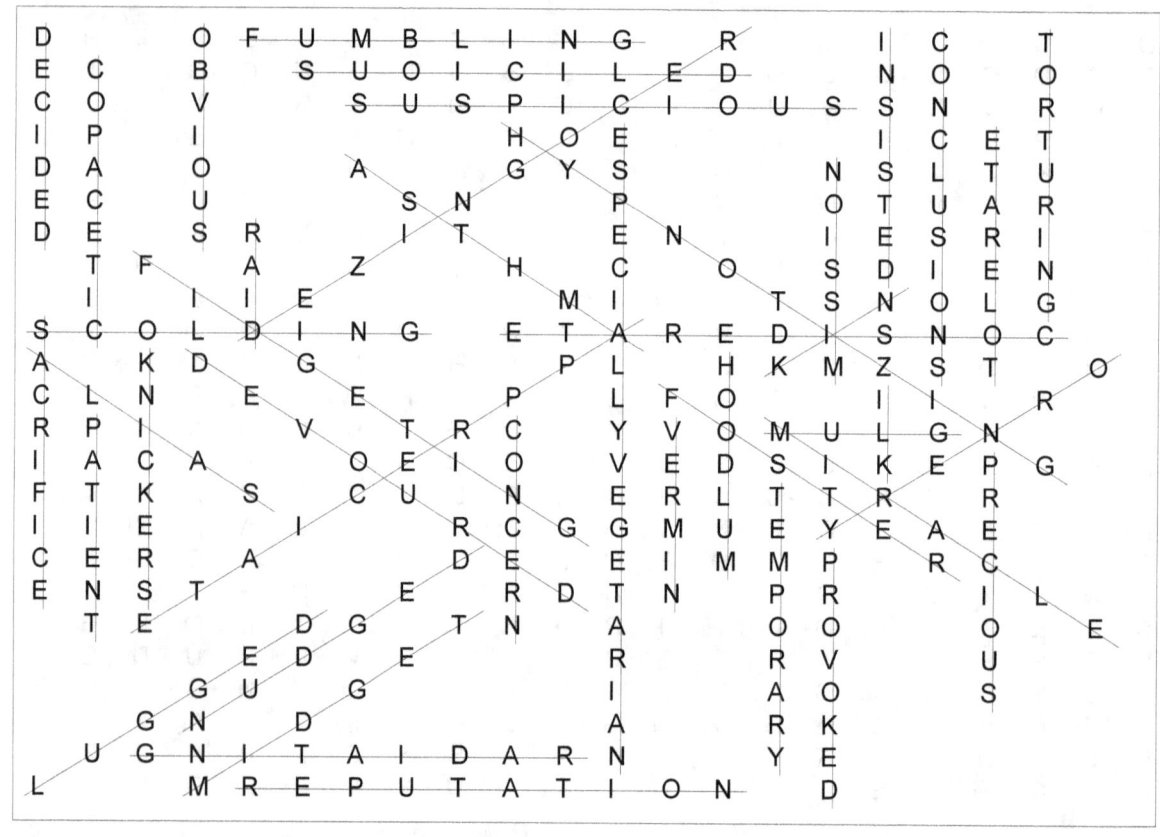

A made-up name usually assumed to hide one's true identity (5)
A person's character observed by others (10)
Able to wait (7)
Act of God; something impossible happens (7)
Ate quickly and completely or hungrily (8)
Attack or invasion, sometimes to uncover something illegal (4)
Carried (6)
Charitable, usually religious, house for helping needy people (7)
Chose (7)
Clumsily searching (8)
Easy to see (7)
Hardship; giving up something (9)
Having the effect of putting one in a trance or asleep (11)
Identified (10)
Illness causing difficulty breathing (6)
Kind, group, set (3)
Lecturing; reprimanding (8)
Lightly or gently pushed (6)
Low life creatures like rats (6)
Mistreating; tormenting; abusing (9)

Nervously moving about or twitching (9)
Not necessarily bad, but a trouble-maker (6)
Not permanent; just for a while (9)
Particularly (10)
Person who doesn't eat meat (10)
Proper (9)
Put up with; endure (8)
Recognize something's value (10)
Relative (3)
Repeatedly demanded (8)
Results, decisions, deductions (11)
Sad (4)
Shining, beaming, giving off rays (9)
Short pants (8)
Small in size (6)
Small-time criminal (7)
Started; induced (8)
Tastes good (9)
Temporary care (6)
Thinking of what will benefit others (11)
Valuable (8)
Wary, not trusting (10)
Worry or care (7)

Bud, Not Buddy Vocabulary Word Search 3

```
P K D E V O U R E D R E P U T A T I O N D
R S E J E F C H M V L R P Z G Z H B I S E
E U K J G R O F S C R U D L V Q V M K A L
C S O V E Z N S A N M T W H M I R F I C I
I P V C T D S R T R F R F O E Z F N R C
O I O A F I E O Y R R T U V S R U Q I I
U C R N R M D K R B Q E S R D B R M V F O
S I P C I P E C T G R P C N I E P B Q I U
B O R E A J R I U M A M S O T M C L W C S
Q U R N N A N R T N E B S G L O I G E T
K S C N M P T K I Z J T O L M N R N D T Z
C R L H I V E E N J N F N S T K I G I E Z
A A L O D X N R G R H Q N Q M D X Z J A D
P D H O G T L M R G T Y W G L M S S E M L
P I C D E E P G A F O N P O N U D G E D L
R A O L T S M K T I L N C Q Y M M Q M S
E T P U H P L L I D E S R W O D Q N D I H
C I A M T E U S T G R M Y D L T A L S S F
I N C S L C G H U E A F R J V M I R M S J
A G E Q S I G W D T T F D A H Q Z Z M I J
T C T A X A E W E I E K H T I I D W I O X
E T I F K L D B I N S I S T E D L D B N D
M L C L W L Q W M G K A T F P B Q K W K G
A G L U M Y R A R O P M E T O R N E R Y D
```

ALIAS	HYPNOTIZING	PRECIOUS
APPRECIATE	ILK	PROVOKED
ASTHMA	INGRATITUDE	RADIATING
CONCERN	INSISTED	RAID
CONSIDERATE	KIN	RECOGNIZED
COPACETIC	KNICKERS	REPUTATION
DECIDED	LUGGED	SACRIFICE
DELICIOUS	MATRIMONIAL	SCOLDING
DEVOURED	MIDGET	SUSPICIOUS
ESPECIALLY	MIRACLE	TEMPERATURE
FIDGETING	MISSION	TEMPORARY
FOSTER	NUDGED	TOLERATE
FUMBLING	OBVIOUS	TORTURING
GLUM	ORNERY	VEGETARIAN
HOODLUM	PATIENT	VERMIN

Bud, Not Buddy Vocabulary Word Search 3 Answer Key

ALIAS	HYPNOTIZING	PRECIOUS
APPRECIATE	ILK	PROVOKED
ASTHMA	INGRATITUDE	RADIATING
CONCERN	INSISTED	RAID
CONSIDERATE	KIN	RECOGNIZED
COPACETIC	KNICKERS	REPUTATION
DECIDED	LUGGED	SACRIFICE
DELICIOUS	MATRIMONIAL	SCOLDING
DEVOURED	MIDGET	SUSPICIOUS
ESPECIALLY	MIRACLE	TEMPERATURE
FIDGETING	MISSION	TEMPORARY
FOSTER	NUDGED	TOLERATE
FUMBLING	OBVIOUS	TORTURING
GLUM	ORNERY	VEGETARIAN
HOODLUM	PATIENT	VERMIN

Bud, Not Buddy Vocabulary Word Search 4

```
C O N C L U S I O N S T O L E R A T E D L
D D H S O S D L R M C E C R G R Y J E Y C
K E V U Z P L Z T N C V U N G E G R K L C
M T C O C G A B D I F T I V N C U F N A M
P A T I E N T C F V A Z H E H O M U I A Q
M I L C D S W I E R I V O G V G I M C I C
J C P E N E R Y E T X X O E Y N S B K C F
F E Q R T C D P O F I Z D T Q I S L E E M
Q R B P A G M N I J K C L A N Z I I R P F
K P V S H E P Z J N Q K U R F E O N S S D
K P T X T Y V Y J V G M M I R D N G J E W
F A W E H B H W N C X R L A D N R P L K T
X I S Z M L S X D M D K A N V W G I C C H
G R D Z L P C T X W B J A T D E C X O L F
G T S G T D O K S S B P L W I I R C N O R
D C G F E B L R U S J T I R O T X M S C E
W R J J H T D O A P O A A U R C U T I O P
R A D I A T I N G R I N S I S T E D D N U
M S N H B V N N T O Y I T T K R C M E C T
K N T Y B G G U G V R K J Q H N D I R E A
H F B O V V R R R O E F M M K M I D A R T
E L C A R I M Q P K N U D G E D A G T N I
Q X D F N W L K N E R Y B G V V R E E K O
L U G G E D Q K Y D O G L U M R Y T Q K N
```

ALIAS
APPRECIATE
ASTHMA
CONCERN
CONCLUSIONS
CONSIDERATE
COPACETIC
DECIDED
DELICIOUS
DEVOURED
ESPECIALLY
FIDGETING
FOSTER
FUMBLING
GLUM

HOODLUM
HYPNOTIZING
ILK
INGRATITUDE
INSISTED
KIN
KNICKERS
LUGGED
MIDGET
MIRACLE
MISSION
NUDGED
OBVIOUS
ORNERY
PATIENT

PRECIOUS
PROVOKED
RADIATING
RAID
RECOGNIZED
REPUTATION
SACRIFICE
SCOLDING
TEMPERATURE
TEMPORARY
TOLERATE
TORTURING
VEGETARIAN
VERMIN

Bud, Not Buddy Vocabulary Word Search 4 Answer Key

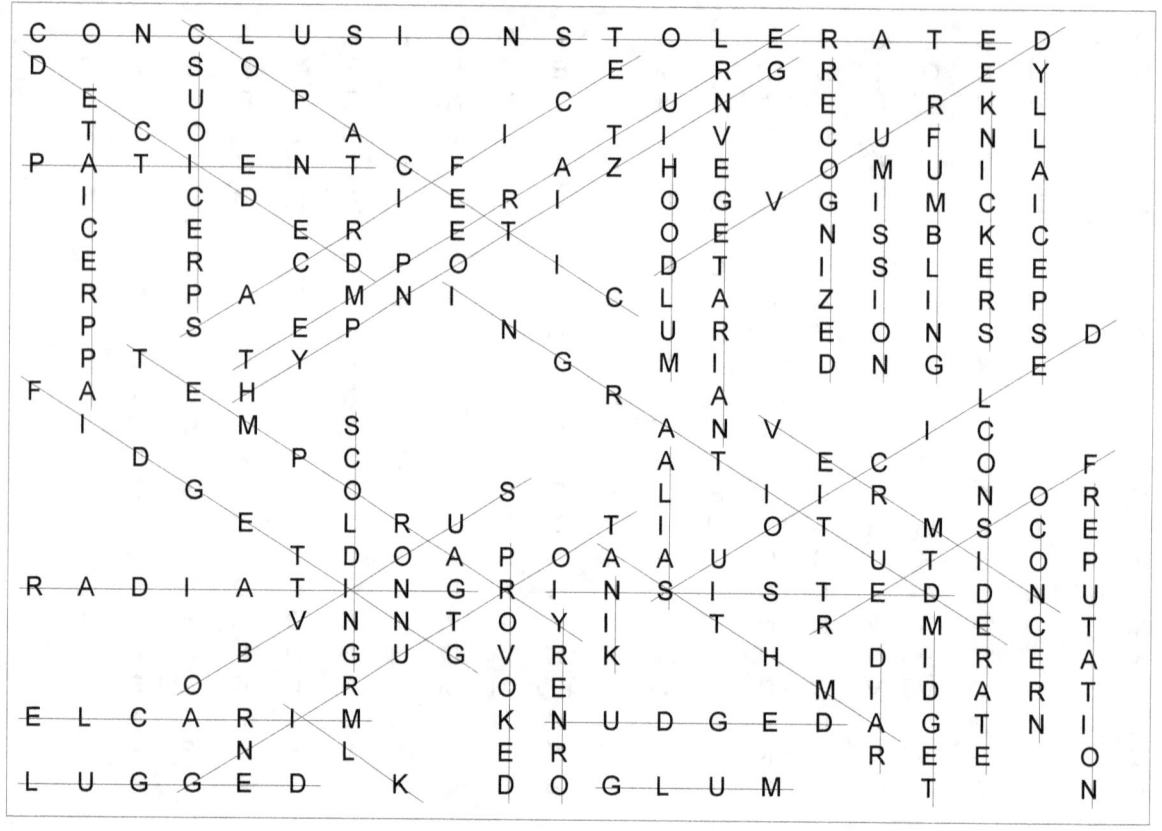

ALIAS	HOODLUM	PRECIOUS
APPRECIATE	HYPNOTIZING	PROVOKED
ASTHMA	ILK	RADIATING
CONCERN	INGRATITUDE	RAID
CONCLUSIONS	INSISTED	RECOGNIZED
CONSIDERATE	KIN	REPUTATION
COPACETIC	KNICKERS	SACRIFICE
DECIDED	LUGGED	SCOLDING
DELICIOUS	MIDGET	TEMPERATURE
DEVOURED	MIRACLE	TEMPORARY
ESPECIALLY	MISSION	TOLERATE
FIDGETING	NUDGED	TORTURING
FOSTER	OBVIOUS	VEGETARIAN
FUMBLING	ORNERY	VERMIN
GLUM	PATIENT	

Bud, Not Buddy Vocabulary Crossword 1

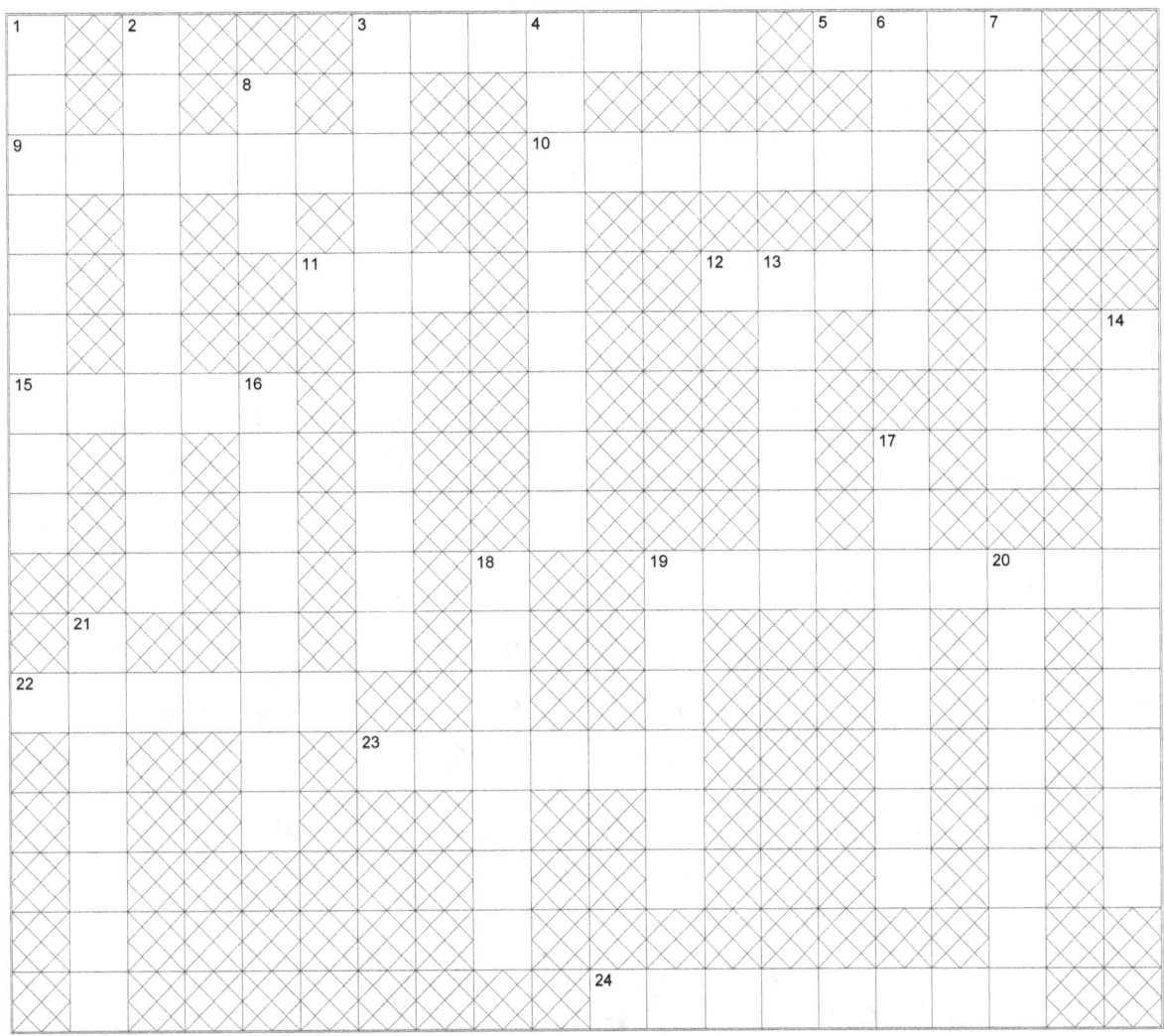

Across
3. Worry or care
5. Attack or invasion, sometimes to uncover something illegal
9. Charitable, usually religious, house for helping needy people
10. Able to wait
11. Kind, group, set
12. Sad
15. A made-up name usually assumed to hide one's true identity
19. Nervously moving about or twitching
22. Low life creatures like rats
23. Small in size
24. Started; induced

Down
1. Not permanent; just for a while
2. Wary, not trusting
3. Results, decisions, deductions
4. Proper
6. Illness causing difficulty breathing
7. Ate quickly and completely or hungrily
8. Relative
13. Carried
14. Identified
16. Lecturing; reprimanding
17. Valuable
18. Small-time criminal
19. Temporary care
20. Repeatedly demanded
21. Chose

Bud, Not Buddy Vocabulary Crossword 1 Answer Key

Across
3. Worry or care
5. Attack or invasion, sometimes to uncover something illegal
9. Charitable, usually religious, house for helping needy people
10. Able to wait
11. Kind, group, set
12. Sad
15. A made-up name usually assumed to hide one's true identity
19. Nervously moving about or twitching
22. Low life creatures like rats
23. Small in size
24. Started; induced

Down
1. Not permanent; just for a while
2. Wary, not trusting
3. Results, decisions, deductions
4. Proper
6. Illness causing difficulty breathing
7. Ate quickly and completely or hungrily
8. Relative
13. Carried
14. Identified
16. Lecturing; reprimanding
17. Valuable
18. Small-time criminal
19. Temporary care
20. Repeatedly demanded
21. Chose

Bud, Not Buddy Vocabulary Crossword 2

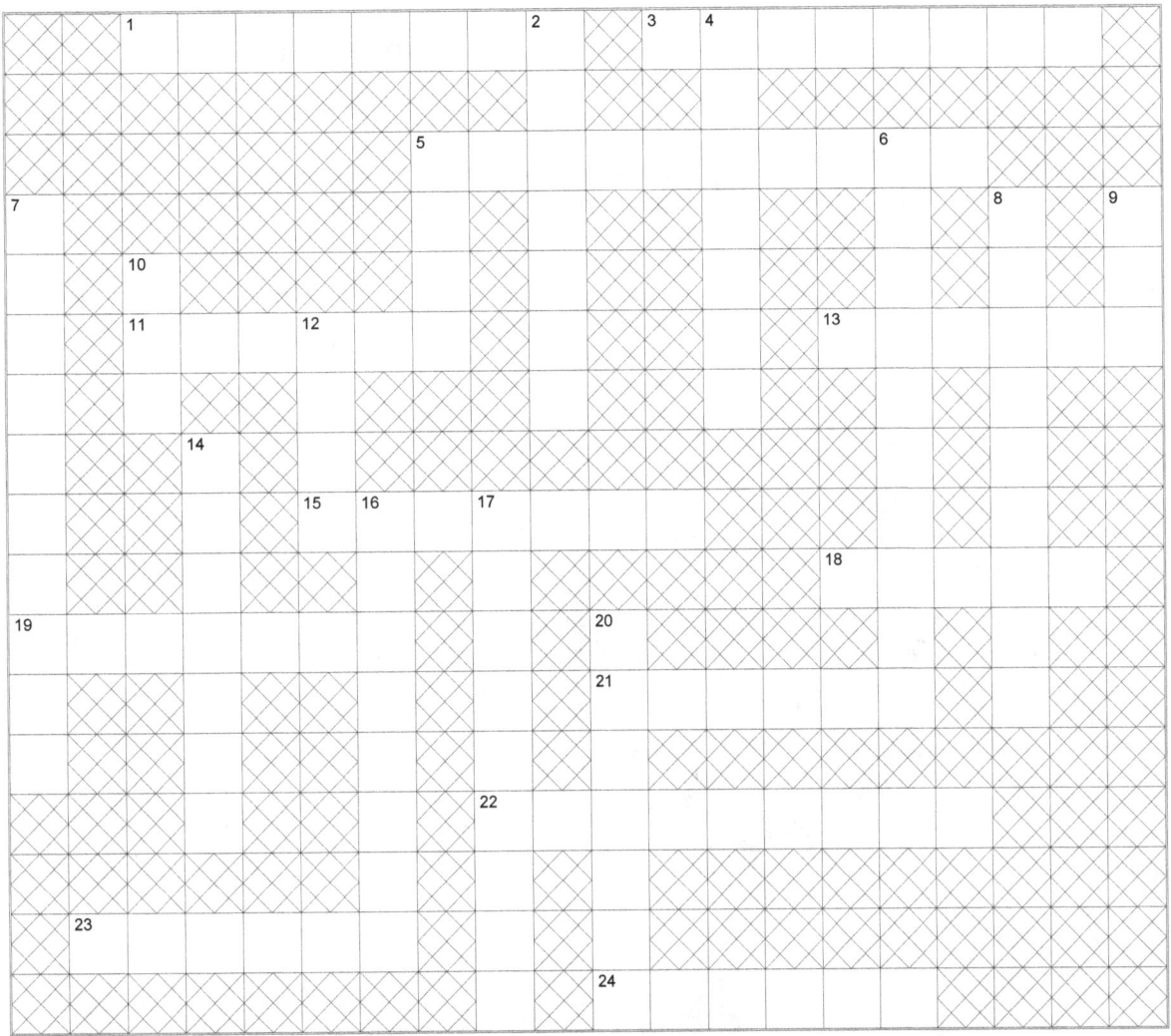

Across
1. Ate quickly and completely or hungrily
3. Lecturing; reprimanding
5. Identified
11. Carried
13. Low life creatures like rats
15. Charitable, usually religious, house for helping needy people
18. A made-up name usually assumed to hide one's true identity
19. Easy to see
21. Not necessarily bad, but a trouble-maker
22. Nervously moving about or twitching
23. Lightly or gently pushed
24. Small in size

Down
2. Chose
4. Worry or care
5. Attack or invasion, sometimes to uncover something illegal
6. Particularly
7. Wary, not trusting
8. Not permanent; just for a while
9. Relative
10. Kind, group, set
12. Sad
14. Able to wait
16. Repeatedly demanded
17. Hardship; giving up something
20. Small-time criminal

Bud, Not Buddy Vocabulary Crossword 2 Answer Key

Across
1. Ate quickly and completely or hungrily
3. Lecturing; reprimanding
5. Identified
11. Carried
13. Low life creatures like rats
15. Charitable, usually religious, house for helping needy people
18. A made-up name usually assumed to hide one's true identity
19. Easy to see
21. Not necessarily bad, but a trouble-maker
22. Nervously moving about or twitching
23. Lightly or gently pushed
24. Small in size

Down
2. Chose
4. Worry or care
5. Attack or invasion, sometimes to uncover something illegal
6. Particularly
7. Wary, not trusting
8. Not permanent; just for a while
9. Relative
10. Kind, group, set
12. Sad
14. Able to wait
16. Repeatedly demanded
17. Hardship; giving up something
20. Small-time criminal

Bud, Not Buddy Vocabulary Crossword 3

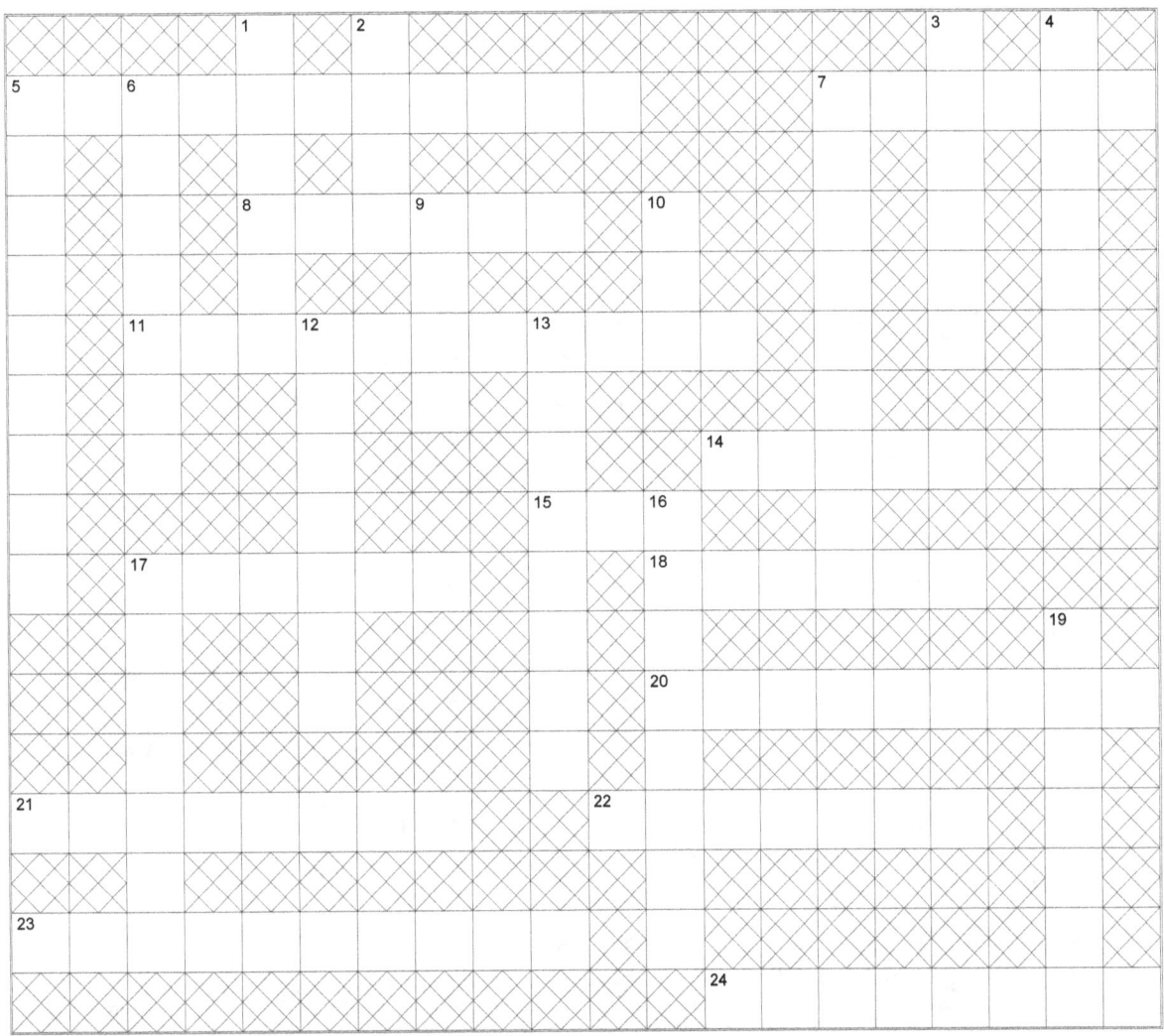

Across
5. Hotness or coldness
7. Temporary care
8. Small in size
11. Results, decisions, deductions
14. A made-up name usually assumed to hide one's true identity
15. Kind, group, set
17. Not necessarily bad, but a trouble-maker
18. Lightly or gently pushed
20. Proper
21. Started; induced
22. Chose
23. Wary, not trusting
24. Clumsily searching

Down
1. Low life creatures like rats
2. Attack or invasion, sometimes to uncover something illegal
3. Illness causing difficulty breathing
4. Ate quickly and completely or hungrily
5. Not permanent; just for a while
6. Act of God; something impossible happens
7. Nervously moving about or twitching
9. Sad
10. Relative
12. Worry or care
13. Repeatedly demanded
16. Short pants
17. Easy to see
19. Charitable, usually religious, house for helping needy people

Bud, Not Buddy Vocabulary Crossword 3 Answer Key

Across
- 5. Hotness or coldness
- 7. Temporary care
- 8. Small in size
- 11. Results, decisions, deductions
- 14. A made-up name usually assumed to hide one's true identity
- 15. Kind, group, set
- 17. Not necessarily bad, but a trouble-maker
- 18. Lightly or gently pushed
- 20. Proper
- 21. Started; induced
- 22. Chose
- 23. Wary, not trusting
- 24. Clumsily searching

Down
- 1. Low life creatures like rats
- 2. Attack or invasion, sometimes to uncover something illegal
- 3. Illness causing difficulty breathing
- 4. Ate quickly and completely or hungrily
- 5. Not permanent; just for a while
- 6. Act of God; something impossible happens
- 7. Nervously moving about or twitching
- 9. Sad
- 10. Relative
- 12. Worry or care
- 13. Repeatedly demanded
- 16. Short pants
- 17. Easy to see
- 19. Charitable, usually religious, house for helping needy people

Bud, Not Buddy Vocabulary Crossword 4

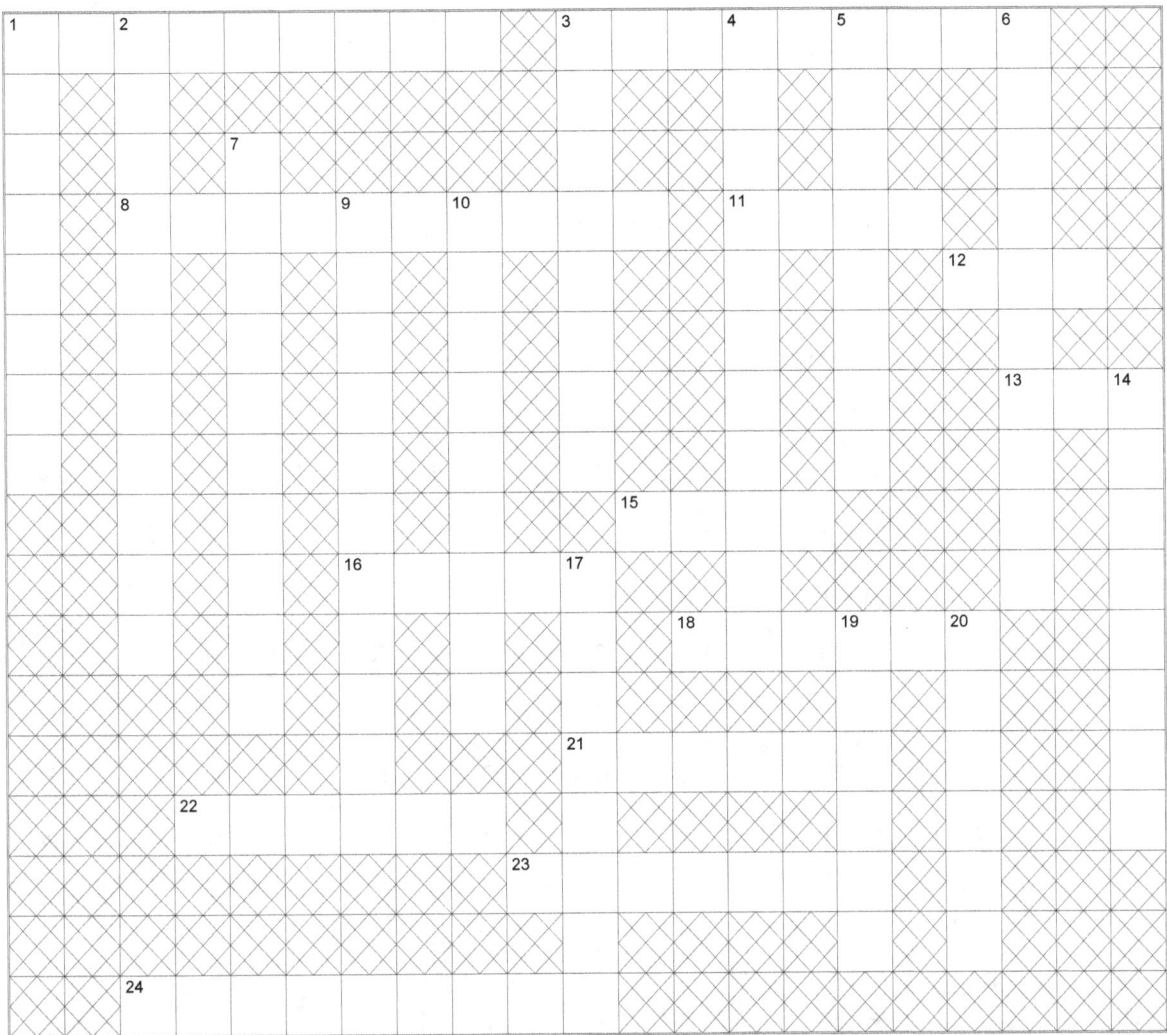

Across
1. Not permanent; just for a while
3. Tastes good
8. A person's character observed by others
11. Attack or invasion, sometimes to uncover something illegal
12. Relative
13. Kind, group, set
15. Sad
16. A made-up name usually assumed to hide one's true identity
18. Low life creatures like rats
21. Carried
22. Not necessarily bad, but a trouble-maker
23. Act of God; something impossible happens
24. Nervously moving about or twitching

Down
1. Put up with; endure
2. Relating to marriage
3. Ate quickly and completely or hungrily
4. Attitude of being not thankful
5. Repeatedly demanded
6. Wary, not trusting
7. Recognize something's value
9. Hotness or coldness
10. Mistreating; tormenting; abusing
14. Short pants
17. Lecturing; reprimanding
19. Small in size
20. Lightly or gently pushed

Bud, Not Buddy Vocabulary Crossword 4 Answer Key

	1 T	E	2 M	P	O	R	A	R	Y		3 D	E	4 L	I	5 C	I	O	6 U	S	
	O		A								E		N		N			U		
	L		T		7 A						V		G		S			S		
	8 E		R	E	P	U	9 T	A	10 T	I	O	N	11 R	A	I	D		P		
	R		I		P		E		O		U		A		S		12 K	I	N	
	A		M		R		M		R		R		T		T		C			
	T		O		E		P		T		E		I		E		13 I	L	14 K	
	E		N		C		E		U		D		T		D		O		N	
			I		I		R		R			15 G	L	U	M		U		I	
			16 A	A	17 A	L	I	A	S				D				S		C	
			L		T		T		C		18 V	E	R	19 M	I	20 N		K	
					E		U		O				I		U				E	
					R				21 L	U	G	G	E	D		D		R	
			22 O	R	N	E	R	Y		D				G		G		S		
								23 M	I	R	A	C	L	E		E			
								N						T		D			
			24 F	I	D	G	E	T	I	N	G								

Across
1. Not permanent; just for a while
3. Tastes good
8. A person's character observed by others
11. Attack or invasion, sometimes to uncover something illegal
12. Relative
13. Kind, group, set
15. Sad
16. A made-up name usually assumed to hide one's true identity
18. Low life creatures like rats
21. Carried
22. Not necessarily bad, but a trouble-maker
23. Act of God; something impossible happens
24. Nervously moving about or twitching

Down
1. Put up with; endure
2. Relating to marriage
3. Ate quickly and completely or hungrily
4. Attitude of being not thankful
5. Repeatedly demanded
6. Wary, not trusting
7. Recognize something's value
9. Hotness or coldness
10. Mistreating; tormenting; abusing
14. Short pants
17. Lecturing; reprimanding
19. Small in size
20. Lightly or gently pushed

Bud, Not Buddy Vocabulary Juggle Letters 1

1. RTIEVEAAGN = 1. _____
   Person who doesn't eat meat

2. GDUDNE = 2. _____
   Lightly or gently pushed

3. KROODEVP = 3. _____
   Started; induced

4. NLOCUIOSCSN = 4. _____
   Results, decisions, deductions

5. IBUSOOV = 5. _____
   Easy to see

6. IUCSOSIPUS = 6. _____
   Wary, not trusting

7. ITHZIONNYGP = 7. _____
   Having the effect of putting one in a trance or asleep

8. RKSKCINE = 8. _____
   Short pants

9. ECPTEAPAIR = 9. _____
   Recognize something's value

10. KIL = 10. _____
    Kind, group, set

11. ULGM = 11. _____
    Sad

12. EUEDRDOV = 12. _____
    Ate quickly and completely or hungrily

13. SDINAEECRTO = 13. _____
    Thinking of what will benefit others

14. UMATEERPRET = 14. _____
    Hotness or coldness

15. SONIMIS = 15. _____
    Charitable, usually religious, house for helping needy people

Bud, Not Buddy Vocabulary Juggle Letters 1 Answer Key

1. RTIEVEAAGN = 1. VEGETARIAN
   Person who doesn't eat meat

2. GDUDNE = 2. NUDGED
   Lightly or gently pushed

3. KROODEVP = 3. PROVOKED
   Started; induced

4. NLOCUIOSCSN = 4. CONCLUSIONS
   Results, decisions, deductions

5. IBUSOOV = 5. OBVIOUS
   Easy to see

6. IUCSOSIPUS = 6. SUSPICIOUS
   Wary, not trusting

7. ITHZIONNYGP = 7. HYPNOTIZING
   Having the effect of putting one in a trance or asleep

8. RKSKCINE = 8. KNICKERS
   Short pants

9. ECPTEAPAIR = 9. APPRECIATE
   Recognize something's value

10. KIL = 10. ILK
    Kind, group, set

11. ULGM = 11. GLUM
    Sad

12. EUEDRDOV = 12. DEVOURED
    Ate quickly and completely or hungrily

13. SDINAEECRTO = 13. CONSIDERATE
    Thinking of what will benefit others

14. UMATEERPRET = 14. TEMPERATURE
    Hotness or coldness

15. SONIMIS = 15. MISSION
    Charitable, usually religious, house for helping needy people

Bud, Not Buddy Vocabulary Juggle Letters 2

1. URDIEITNTAG = 1. _____
   Attitude of being not thankful

2. KDEORVPO = 2. _____
   Started; induced

3. SDOIEICUL = 3. _____
   Tastes good

4. UILOOSCCNSN = 4. _____
   Results, decisions, deductions

5. IAIRNOMMTLA = 5. _____
   Relating to marriage

6. ETFSOR = 6. _____
   Temporary care

7. LGMU = 7. _____
   Sad

8. ECEDDID = 8. _____
   Chose

9. NDIZREOGCE = 9. _____
   Identified

10. UGDELG = 10. _____
    Carried

11. ECNCNOR = 11. _____
    Worry or care

12. OSDINCGL = 12. _____
    Lecturing; reprimanding

13. KECSIRNK = 13. _____
    Short pants

14. IRDA = 14. _____
    Attack or invasion, sometimes to uncover something illegal

15. ILEAYCSEPL = 15. _____
    Particularly

Bud, Not Buddy Vocabulary Juggle Letters 2 Answer Key

1. URDIEITNTAG = 1. INGRATITUDE
Attitude of being not thankful

2. KDEORVPO = 2. PROVOKED
Started; induced

3. SDOIEICUL = 3. DELICIOUS
Tastes good

4. UILOOSCCNSN = 4. CONCLUSIONS
Results, decisions, deductions

5. IAIRNOMMTLA = 5. MATRIMONIAL
Relating to marriage

6. ETFSOR = 6. FOSTER
Temporary care

7. LGMU = 7. GLUM
Sad

8. ECEDDID = 8. DECIDED
Chose

9. NDIZREOGCE = 9. RECOGNIZED
Identified

10. UGDELG = 10. LUGGED
Carried

11. ECNCNOR = 11. CONCERN
Worry or care

12. OSDINCGL = 12. SCOLDING
Lecturing; reprimanding

13. KECSIRNK = 13. KNICKERS
Short pants

14. IRDA = 14. RAID
Attack or invasion, sometimes to uncover something illegal

15. ILEAYCSEPL = 15. ESPECIALLY
Particularly

Bud, Not Buddy Vocabulary Juggle Letters 3

1. GEDDNU = 1. _____
   Lightly or gently pushed

2. NKI = 2. _____
   Relative

3. OMLRAANTMII = 3. _____
   Relating to marriage

4. CUSIIOSUPS = 4. _____
   Wary, not trusting

5. ULMG = 5. _____
   Sad

6. TOERSF = 6. _____
   Temporary care

7. SSEINDTI = 7. _____
   Repeatedly demanded

8. ZHYINPNITOG = 8. _____
   Having the effect of putting one in a trance or asleep

9. USTILROQINVET = 9. _____
   Performer who can make the voice appear to come from somewhere else

10. NUCSLOCNISO = 10. _____
    Results, decisions, deductions

11. LEAOTRET = 11. _____
    Put up with; endure

12. ICSLGNDO = 12. _____
    Lecturing; reprimanding

13. LSEIYPCELA = 13. _____
    Particularly

14. AINRDTGAI = 14. _____
    Shining, beaming, giving off rays

15. HAAMST = 15. _____
    Illness causing difficulty breathing

Bud, Not Buddy Vocabulary Juggle Letters 3 Answer Key

1. GEDDNU = 1. NUDGED
   Lightly or gently pushed

2. NKI = 2. KIN
   Relative

3. OMLRAANTMII = 3. MATRIMONIAL
   Relating to marriage

4. CUSIIOSUPS = 4. SUSPICIOUS
   Wary, not trusting

5. ULMG = 5. GLUM
   Sad

6. TOERSF = 6. FOSTER
   Temporary care

7. SSEINDTI = 7. INSISTED
   Repeatedly demanded

8. ZHYINPNITOG = 8. HYPNOTIZING
   Having the effect of putting one in a trance or asleep

9. USTILROQINVET = 9. VENTRILOQUIST
   Performer who can make the voice appear to come from somewhere else

10. NUCSLOCNISO = 10. CONCLUSIONS
    Results, decisions, deductions

11. LEAOTRET = 11. TOLERATE
    Put up with; endure

12. ICSLGNDO = 12. SCOLDING
    Lecturing; reprimanding

13. LSEIYPCELA = 13. ESPECIALLY
    Particularly

14. AINRDTGAI = 14. RADIATING
    Shining, beaming, giving off rays

15. HAAMST = 15. ASTHMA
    Illness causing difficulty breathing

Bud, Not Buddy Vocabulary Juggle Letters 4

1. LUMG = 1. _____
   Sad

2. NOAPTIREUT = 2. _____
   A person's character observed by others

3. EPLEISALCY = 3. _____
   Particularly

4. EMERTPUEATR = 4. _____
   Hotness or coldness

5. YARMPERTO = 5. _____
   Not permanent; just for a while

6. TSITLRNUEVIOQ = 6. _____
   Performer who can make the voice appear to come from somewhere else

7. RNITUGORT = 7. _____
   Mistreating; tormenting; abusing

8. IPUOERCS = 8. _____
   Valuable

9. UIOPIUSSSC = 9. _____
   Wary, not trusting

10. ECORNNC =10. _____
    Worry or care

11. GDUNED =11. _____
    Lightly or gently pushed

12. GULEDG =12. _____
    Carried

13. CRDNIEGZOE =13. _____
    Identified

14. EAGNRITDIUT =14. _____
    Attitude of being not thankful

15. DCOLISGN =15. _____
    Lecturing; reprimanding

Bud, Not Buddy Vocabulary Juggle Letters 4 Answer Key

1. LUMG = 1. GLUM
Sad

2. NOAPTIREUT = 2. REPUTATION
A person's character observed by others

3. EPLEISALCY = 3. ESPECIALLY
Particularly

4. EMERTPUEATR = 4. TEMPERATURE
Hotness or coldness

5. YARMPERTO = 5. TEMPORARY
Not permanent; just for a while

6. TSITLRNUEVIOQ = 6. VENTRILOQUIST
Performer who can make the voice appear to come from somewhere else

7. RNITUGORT = 7. TORTURING
Mistreating; tormenting; abusing

8. IPUOERCS = 8. PRECIOUS
Valuable

9. UIOPIUSSSC = 9. SUSPICIOUS
Wary, not trusting

10. ECORNNC = 10. CONCERN
Worry or care

11. GDUNED = 11. NUDGED
Lightly or gently pushed

12. GULEDG = 12. LUGGED
Carried

13. CRDNIEGZOE = 13. RECOGNIZED
Identified

14. EAGNRITDIUT = 14. INGRATITUDE
Attitude of being not thankful

15. DCOLISGN = 15. SCOLDING
Lecturing; reprimanding

ALIAS	A made-up name usually assumed to hide one's true identity
APPRECIATE	Recognize something's value
ASTHMA	Illness causing difficulty breathing
CONCERN	Worry or care
CONCLUSIONS	Results, decisions, deductions
CONSIDERATE	Thinking of what will benefit others

COPACETIC	Proper
DECIDED	Chose
DELICIOUS	Tastes good
DEVOURED	Ate quickly and completely or hungrily
ESPECIALLY	Particularly
FIDGETING	Nervously moving about or twitching

FOSTER	Temporary care
FUMBLING	Clumsily searching
GLUM	Sad
HOODLUM	Small-time criminal
HYPNOTIZING	Having the effect of putting one in a trance or asleep
ILK	Kind, group, set

INGRATITUDE	Attitude of being not thankful
INSISTED	Repeatedly demanded
KIN	Relative
KNICKERS	Short pants
LUGGED	Carried
MATRIMONIAL	Relating to marriage

MIDGET	Small in size
MIRACLE	Act of God; something impossible happens
MISSION	Charitable, usually religious, house for helping needy people
NUDGED	Lightly or gently pushed
OBVIOUS	Easy to see
ORNERY	Not necessarily bad, but a trouble-maker

PATIENT	Able to wait
PRECIOUS	Valuable
PROVOKED	Started; induced
RADIATING	Shining, beaming, giving off rays
RAID	Attack or invasion, sometimes to uncover something illegal
RECOGNIZED	Identified

REPUTATION	A person's character observed by others
SACRIFICE	Hardship; giving up something
SCOLDING	Lecturing; reprimanding
SUSPICIOUS	Wary, not trusting
TEMPERATURE	Hotness or coldness
TEMPORARY	Not permanent; just for a while

TOLERATE	Put up with; endure
TORTURING	Mistreating; tormenting; abusing
VEGETARIAN	Person who doesn't eat meat
VENTRILOQUIST	Performer who can make the voice appear to come from somewhere else
VERMIN	Low life creatures like rats

Bud, Not Buddy Vocabulary

VEGETARIAN	FOSTER	ESPECIALLY	ORNERY	GLUM
RADIATING	APPRECIATE	ASTHMA	TEMPERATURE	LUGGED
VERMIN	CONSIDERATE	FREE SPACE	CONCLUSIONS	VENTRILOQUIST
RECOGNIZED	PRECIOUS	MIRACLE	SACRIFICE	DEVOURED
DELICIOUS	RAID	INSISTED	PATIENT	KNICKERS

Bud, Not Buddy Vocabulary

MATRIMONIAL	HOODLUM	OBVIOUS	TOLERATE	REPUTATION
INGRATITUDE	MISSION	TORTURING	DECIDED	FUMBLING
SUSPICIOUS	KIN	FREE SPACE	NUDGED	CONCERN
MIDGET	ILK	FIDGETING	SCOLDING	ALIAS
HYPNOTIZING	PROVOKED	KNICKERS	PATIENT	INSISTED

Bud, Not Buddy Vocabulary

FIDGETING	DELICIOUS	TOLERATE	PATIENT	MIDGET
CONCERN	PRECIOUS	MIRACLE	RADIATING	SCOLDING
VENTRILOQUIST	CONCLUSIONS	FREE SPACE	TEMPORARY	GLUM
ALIAS	DECIDED	ESPECIALLY	HOODLUM	PROVOKED
TEMPERATURE	MISSION	OBVIOUS	FOSTER	DEVOURED

Bud, Not Buddy Vocabulary

COPACETIC	RAID	VEGETARIAN	TORTURING	NUDGED
LUGGED	ASTHMA	FUMBLING	KIN	SUSPICIOUS
CONSIDERATE	VERMIN	FREE SPACE	INGRATITUDE	SACRIFICE
REPUTATION	RECOGNIZED	MATRIMONIAL	HYPNOTIZING	INSISTED
APPRECIATE	KNICKERS	DEVOURED	FOSTER	OBVIOUS

Bud, Not Buddy Vocabulary

CONSIDERATE	VERMIN	FOSTER	APPRECIATE	INGRATITUDE
PATIENT	ILK	TEMPORARY	SCOLDING	RECOGNIZED
DECIDED	FUMBLING	FREE SPACE	MATRIMONIAL	RADIATING
TOLERATE	REPUTATION	RAID	LUGGED	ALIAS
CONCERN	DELICIOUS	PROVOKED	COPACETIC	OBVIOUS

Bud, Not Buddy Vocabulary

PRECIOUS	HOODLUM	MIRACLE	NUDGED	CONCLUSIONS
TEMPERATURE	MIDGET	VENTRILOQUIST	DEVOURED	KNICKERS
ESPECIALLY	SACRIFICE	FREE SPACE	MISSION	ASTHMA
SUSPICIOUS	KIN	TORTURING	GLUM	INSISTED
VEGETARIAN	HYPNOTIZING	OBVIOUS	COPACETIC	PROVOKED

Bud, Not Buddy Vocabulary

NUDGED	MIRACLE	PRECIOUS	ASTHMA	ESPECIALLY
SCOLDING	MATRIMONIAL	INSISTED	COPACETIC	HYPNOTIZING
MIDGET	LUGGED	FREE SPACE	RAID	PATIENT
SUSPICIOUS	REPUTATION	OBVIOUS	CONCLUSIONS	DELICIOUS
VENTRILOQUIST	FOSTER	ORNERY	TORTURING	DEVOURED

Bud, Not Buddy Vocabulary

HOODLUM	INGRATITUDE	GLUM	FUMBLING	PROVOKED
RECOGNIZED	APPRECIATE	MISSION	FIDGETING	CONCERN
ILK	VEGETARIAN	FREE SPACE	TOLERATE	TEMPERATURE
RADIATING	CONSIDERATE	KNICKERS	SACRIFICE	DECIDED
ALIAS	VERMIN	DEVOURED	TORTURING	ORNERY

Bud, Not Buddy Vocabulary

FIDGETING	INSISTED	RADIATING	SACRIFICE	FUMBLING
CONCERN	CONCLUSIONS	DELICIOUS	MIDGET	TOLERATE
REPUTATION	ORNERY	FREE SPACE	VEGETARIAN	NUDGED
MIRACLE	TEMPORARY	ASTHMA	ESPECIALLY	SCOLDING
VENTRILOQUIST	COPACETIC	KNICKERS	MISSION	INGRATITUDE

Bud, Not Buddy Vocabulary

PATIENT	TEMPERATURE	ALIAS	TORTURING	DECIDED
ILK	RECOGNIZED	CONSIDERATE	LUGGED	PRECIOUS
DEVOURED	FOSTER	FREE SPACE	APPRECIATE	MATRIMONIAL
SUSPICIOUS	KIN	RAID	HOODLUM	HYPNOTIZING
PROVOKED	VERMIN	INGRATITUDE	MISSION	KNICKERS

Bud, Not Buddy Vocabulary

FIDGETING	REPUTATION	ESPECIALLY	DELICIOUS	DECIDED
RAID	VERMIN	ASTHMA	SUSPICIOUS	HOODLUM
ORNERY	LUGGED	FREE SPACE	ILK	MIDGET
CONCERN	RADIATING	COPACETIC	PROVOKED	TEMPORARY
MIRACLE	APPRECIATE	HYPNOTIZING	FOSTER	GLUM

Bud, Not Buddy Vocabulary

CONCLUSIONS	VENTRILOQUIST	INSISTED	SACRIFICE	TORTURING
PRECIOUS	OBVIOUS	TEMPERATURE	FUMBLING	NUDGED
PATIENT	ALIAS	FREE SPACE	MATRIMONIAL	INGRATITUDE
KNICKERS	DEVOURED	SCOLDING	MISSION	CONSIDERATE
VEGETARIAN	KIN	GLUM	FOSTER	HYPNOTIZING

Bud, Not Buddy Vocabulary

ASTHMA	ESPECIALLY	FUMBLING	RECOGNIZED	MATRIMONIAL
PATIENT	MIDGET	DEVOURED	PROVOKED	DELICIOUS
SCOLDING	NUDGED	FREE SPACE	VERMIN	INGRATITUDE
SACRIFICE	LUGGED	ORNERY	ILK	DECIDED
KNICKERS	INSISTED	CONCLUSIONS	MISSION	VENTRILOQUIST

Bud, Not Buddy Vocabulary

REPUTATION	KIN	PRECIOUS	TEMPERATURE	HYPNOTIZING
SUSPICIOUS	APPRECIATE	TORTURING	HOODLUM	TOLERATE
TEMPORARY	COPACETIC	FREE SPACE	RADIATING	CONCERN
CONSIDERATE	MIRACLE	OBVIOUS	GLUM	FOSTER
VEGETARIAN	ALIAS	VENTRILOQUIST	MISSION	CONCLUSIONS

Bud, Not Buddy Vocabulary

APPRECIATE	RADIATING	PRECIOUS	ILK	MISSION
SUSPICIOUS	CONSIDERATE	CONCLUSIONS	REPUTATION	DECIDED
SACRIFICE	NUDGED	FREE SPACE	INSISTED	KIN
FOSTER	ESPECIALLY	DELICIOUS	ASTHMA	INGRATITUDE
FUMBLING	MIRACLE	TORTURING	LUGGED	TOLERATE

Bud, Not Buddy Vocabulary

COPACETIC	PROVOKED	OBVIOUS	RECOGNIZED	KNICKERS
HYPNOTIZING	FIDGETING	MATRIMONIAL	VERMIN	ALIAS
TEMPERATURE	RAID	FREE SPACE	GLUM	ORNERY
PATIENT	DEVOURED	SCOLDING	VEGETARIAN	HOODLUM
MIDGET	VENTRILOQUIST	TOLERATE	LUGGED	TORTURING

Bud, Not Buddy Vocabulary

FOSTER	FUMBLING	REPUTATION	NUDGED	DELICIOUS
MIRACLE	DEVOURED	APPRECIATE	LUGGED	TOLERATE
MATRIMONIAL	RADIATING	FREE SPACE	SUSPICIOUS	SACRIFICE
ALIAS	PATIENT	COPACETIC	CONSIDERATE	HYPNOTIZING
VENTRILOQUIST	TORTURING	GLUM	VEGETARIAN	INGRATITUDE

Bud, Not Buddy Vocabulary

ASTHMA	KIN	VERMIN	DECIDED	PRECIOUS
SCOLDING	MISSION	INSISTED	CONCERN	KNICKERS
OBVIOUS	TEMPORARY	FREE SPACE	PROVOKED	RAID
HOODLUM	MIDGET	CONCLUSIONS	RECOGNIZED	ESPECIALLY
ORNERY	FIDGETING	INGRATITUDE	VEGETARIAN	GLUM

Bud, Not Buddy Vocabulary

INSISTED	CONCERN	RADIATING	REPUTATION	KNICKERS
MIRACLE	ORNERY	HYPNOTIZING	PRECIOUS	TEMPORARY
MATRIMONIAL	PATIENT	FREE SPACE	RAID	CONCLUSIONS
PROVOKED	SACRIFICE	TOLERATE	ALIAS	VERMIN
APPRECIATE	CONSIDERATE	VENTRILOQUIST	LUGGED	OBVIOUS

Bud, Not Buddy Vocabulary

TORTURING	GLUM	HOODLUM	FOSTER	FIDGETING
MISSION	ASTHMA	ILK	DECIDED	INGRATITUDE
RECOGNIZED	MIDGET	FREE SPACE	SUSPICIOUS	VEGETARIAN
FUMBLING	SCOLDING	DEVOURED	COPACETIC	DELICIOUS
TEMPERATURE	ESPECIALLY	OBVIOUS	LUGGED	VENTRILOQUIST

Bud, Not Buddy Vocabulary

TEMPERATURE	PRECIOUS	KNICKERS	MIRACLE	SUSPICIOUS
RADIATING	COPACETIC	DEVOURED	DECIDED	PROVOKED
TEMPORARY	RECOGNIZED	FREE SPACE	MIDGET	INGRATITUDE
VERMIN	DELICIOUS	MATRIMONIAL	TOLERATE	ORNERY
SCOLDING	TORTURING	RAID	APPRECIATE	GLUM

Bud, Not Buddy Vocabulary

OBVIOUS	REPUTATION	ALIAS	HOODLUM	VEGETARIAN
FIDGETING	NUDGED	SACRIFICE	VENTRILOQUIST	INSISTED
LUGGED	KIN	FREE SPACE	ESPECIALLY	CONCLUSIONS
MISSION	PATIENT	HYPNOTIZING	ILK	FUMBLING
CONCERN	FOSTER	GLUM	APPRECIATE	RAID

Bud, Not Buddy Vocabulary

VENTRILOQUIST	MIRACLE	CONCERN	INGRATITUDE	ASTHMA
RAID	CONSIDERATE	INSISTED	PATIENT	FIDGETING
ESPECIALLY	SACRIFICE	FREE SPACE	TEMPERATURE	GLUM
TEMPORARY	MIDGET	CONCLUSIONS	SUSPICIOUS	RADIATING
SCOLDING	KIN	MISSION	FOSTER	RECOGNIZED

Bud, Not Buddy Vocabulary

HYPNOTIZING	TOLERATE	ALIAS	DEVOURED	VERMIN
DECIDED	REPUTATION	OBVIOUS	ILK	ORNERY
NUDGED	APPRECIATE	FREE SPACE	PROVOKED	DELICIOUS
TORTURING	HOODLUM	MATRIMONIAL	PRECIOUS	KNICKERS
LUGGED	FUMBLING	RECOGNIZED	FOSTER	MISSION

Bud, Not Buddy Vocabulary

VENTRILOQUIST	HYPNOTIZING	OBVIOUS	DECIDED	ESPECIALLY
INGRATITUDE	VEGETARIAN	TOLERATE	VERMIN	DEVOURED
INSISTED	RADIATING	FREE SPACE	PRECIOUS	CONSIDERATE
CONCERN	RAID	RECOGNIZED	REPUTATION	KNICKERS
CONCLUSIONS	ILK	ALIAS	FUMBLING	SCOLDING

Bud, Not Buddy Vocabulary

APPRECIATE	DELICIOUS	SACRIFICE	GLUM	FIDGETING
MIDGET	PATIENT	MIRACLE	MATRIMONIAL	ASTHMA
MISSION	COPACETIC	FREE SPACE	TORTURING	ORNERY
SUSPICIOUS	TEMPERATURE	FOSTER	TEMPORARY	NUDGED
PROVOKED	LUGGED	SCOLDING	FUMBLING	ALIAS

Bud, Not Buddy Vocabulary

GLUM	PRECIOUS	NUDGED	TOLERATE	DELICIOUS
MIRACLE	SUSPICIOUS	PATIENT	ORNERY	FOSTER
KIN	INGRATITUDE	FREE SPACE	OBVIOUS	DEVOURED
PROVOKED	TEMPERATURE	MIDGET	TEMPORARY	DECIDED
VERMIN	CONCLUSIONS	SACRIFICE	VEGETARIAN	RAID

Bud, Not Buddy Vocabulary

SCOLDING	APPRECIATE	ESPECIALLY	COPACETIC	INSISTED
HOODLUM	MISSION	RECOGNIZED	TORTURING	VENTRILOQUIST
HYPNOTIZING	ILK	FREE SPACE	FIDGETING	ALIAS
REPUTATION	CONSIDERATE	KNICKERS	CONCERN	LUGGED
FUMBLING	MATRIMONIAL	RAID	VEGETARIAN	SACRIFICE

Bud, Not Buddy Vocabulary

TEMPERATURE	PRECIOUS	FOSTER	GLUM	FUMBLING
CONSIDERATE	VERMIN	SCOLDING	CONCLUSIONS	MIDGET
COPACETIC	MIRACLE	FREE SPACE	INGRATITUDE	DELICIOUS
VEGETARIAN	NUDGED	CONCERN	KIN	ASTHMA
RAID	MISSION	PROVOKED	REPUTATION	ESPECIALLY

Bud, Not Buddy Vocabulary

MATRIMONIAL	ALIAS	VENTRILOQUIST	APPRECIATE	ILK
RECOGNIZED	LUGGED	DECIDED	FIDGETING	HYPNOTIZING
KNICKERS	INSISTED	FREE SPACE	OBVIOUS	SUSPICIOUS
SACRIFICE	TEMPORARY	PATIENT	ORNERY	HOODLUM
DEVOURED	RADIATING	ESPECIALLY	REPUTATION	PROVOKED

Bud, Not Buddy Vocabulary

CONCLUSIONS	ILK	LUGGED	RECOGNIZED	KIN
TOLERATE	COPACETIC	NUDGED	OBVIOUS	ASTHMA
SCOLDING	TEMPERATURE	FREE SPACE	FOSTER	SACRIFICE
ORNERY	HOODLUM	SUSPICIOUS	VENTRILOQUIST	PATIENT
MATRIMONIAL	PRECIOUS	FUMBLING	VERMIN	INSISTED

Bud, Not Buddy Vocabulary

ESPECIALLY	FIDGETING	MISSION	KNICKERS	APPRECIATE
HYPNOTIZING	MIRACLE	DELICIOUS	GLUM	TORTURING
MIDGET	VEGETARIAN	FREE SPACE	ALIAS	CONCERN
RAID	CONSIDERATE	TEMPORARY	DEVOURED	PROVOKED
INGRATITUDE	DECIDED	INSISTED	VERMIN	FUMBLING